Praise

Don't Lead Alone

"By sharing their collective experience and wisdom, Cleveland Justis and Daniel Student have created a road map to finding big-picture, creative solutions to seemingly unsolvable business problems. It is this type of thinking that I brought to my work at Joie de Vivre and then as Head of Global Hospitality and Strategy at Airbnb. I wasn't born with the skills to solve big challenges. I learned them over time. You can too. This is a must-read for any leader."

—CHIP CONLEY, *New York Times* best-selling author and former Head of Global Hospitality and Strategy, Airbnb

"*Don't Lead Alone* provides leaders with a broad range of tools to tackle complex problems across sectors and geographies. It shows how innovators can build and enhance skills like curiosity, systems mapping, and empathetic listening to see challenges and possible solutions in new ways and to build complex partnerships with new allies to incorporate a greater array of ideas, experiences, and wisdom. A great resource for leaders seeking to solve the hard problems of our time."

—ANNE MARIE BURGOYNE, Managing Director, Philanthropy, Emerson Collective

"Cleveland Justis and Daniel Student bring their decades of experience as organizational leaders, business developers, and builders of successful private companies and nonprofits to *Don't Lead Alone*, a detailed and perceptive exploration of innovation, collaboration, and creative leadership. They invite us into the worlds of leaders who have approached complex challenges with originality and vision, building successful startups and extraordinary partnerships along the way. At the same time, they guide us toward a comprehensive understanding and expression of our own leadership practices and principles, sharing the insight, inspiration, and wisdom needed to help us take our entrepreneurial ideas and collaborative skills to the next level."

—GARY MAY, Chancellor, University of California, Davis

"The world we know is converging and multisectoral—but until now, we haven't identified the skills leaders need to pioneer this new territory. *Don't Lead Alone* (gratefully based on real leaders doing real work) is mapping the way for emerging leaders, changemakers, and their teachers in schools and leadership development programs everywhere. Thank you, Cleve and Daniel."

—NORA SILVER, Founder and Faculty Director, Center for Social Sector Leadership, Haas School of Business, University of California, Berkeley

"Cleve and his team have helped us navigate challenges and find creative solutions to entrenched problems through collaboration with business, government, and nonprofit partners. This journey isn't always easy, but they open your eyes to new ways of looking at things and to see the potential to change, innovate, and ultimately find your own best path forward. *Don't Lead Alone* will help you tremendously in your journey."

—JON JARVIS, Director (retired), National Park Service

"*Don't Lead Alone: Think Like a System, Act Like a Network, and Lead Like a Movement* charts a path forward for bringing together business, government, and nonprofits to solve our most critical social problems while simultaneously driving innovation. Highly recommended for all leaders, entrepreneurs, and change agents."

—RANDI FISHER, Co-Founder and Trustee, Pisces Foundation

"Cleveland and Daniel have been consultants to Outdoor Afro for nearly a decade. But they are also something more. They have a unique way of seeing my strengths and reflecting my own voice and thoughts back to me so I'll truly hear them. I'm not surprised they wrote a book on the skills you need to partner. Because that's what they are in real life: partners to us and to our field of leaders widely."

—RUE MAPP, Founder and CEO, Outdoor Afro

"Are you looking for ways that your organization can work efficiently to drive meaningful social change? If so, *Don't Lead Alone* by Cleveland Justis and Daniel Student can provide helpful tools and examples to do just that."

—STEVE SCHROEDER, CEO (retired), Robert Wood Johnson Foundation

"The challenges we face as a community, as a nation, and as a planet cannot be addressed by any one entity or sector. We must lean on the diverse strength of cross-sector collaborations that engage the systemic challenges that threaten our ability to thrive. Cleve and Daniel have provided a road map for anyone in any organization to recognize the power they hold to make this change. I know that leadership is an activity and not a role; anyone can learn to 'lead like a movement.' Please explore the invitation that they offer. The world needs each one of us."

—BILL COY, Director, Omidyar Fellows Program

"Building quality health care in underdeveloped and under-resourced countries relies on training our doctors, nurses, and hospital staff to work with their communities. It's rare that a book speaks directly to my work, but *Don't Lead Alone* recognizes that to tackle systems-level change, we need to build a robust network of academic, public sector, foundation, and corporate partners. The skills our teams need go beyond the operating room; we have to learn to listen, collaborate, and build trust. *Don't Lead Alone* provides a road map to tackle big change through individual, small actions. Each chapter contains insightful wisdom that we all need to become transformational leaders."

—ANATOLE MANZI, Deputy Chief Medical Officer and Director, Global Learning Collaborative, Partners in Health

"*Don't Lead Alone* is critical reading for anyone who seeks to tackle big, complex problems. Through practical skill development, relevant case studies, and useful frameworks, Justis and Student have given us an engaging and useful guide to next-level leadership. The book also recategorizes leadership away from the notion of solitary hero toward the more impactful model of collaborative, cross-sectoral leadership. I highly recommend this book."

—LIZ MAW, President, Presidio Graduate School

"Large, isolated, optimized organizations were maybe successful pre-COVID. Now, with painful clarity, we see the need to step not just out of organizational silos but out of our industry-niche silos. We wax poetic about the complexity of our problems and the importance of our partnerships—but how do we translate our thinking into action? These authors have lived that work for many years, and I am excited to explore the skills they introduce as we lead meaningful work into a new era."

—TERRI WATSON, President, National Outdoor Leadership School

DON'T LEAD ALONE

THINK LIKE A SYSTEM, ACT LIKE A NETWORK, LEAD LIKE A MOVEMENT!

CLEVELAND JUSTIS, PHD, MBA
& DANIEL STUDENT, MBA

FC

**FAST
COMPANY**
Press

Fast Company Press
New York, New York
www.fastcompanypress.com

This work is being published under the Fast Company Press imprint by an exclusive arrangement with *Fast Company*. *Fast Company* and the *Fast Company* logo are registered trademarks of Mansueto Ventures, LLC. The Fast Company Press logo is a wholly owned trademark of Mansueto Ventures, LLC.

Distributed by River Grove Books

Design and composition by Greenleaf Book Group and Kim Lance
Cover design by Greenleaf Book Group and Kim Lance

Publisher's Cataloging-in-Publication data is available.

Print ISBN: 978-1-63908-040-3

eBook ISBN: 978-1-63908-041-0

First Edition

WE'D LIKE TO DEDICATE THIS BOOK TO OUR FAMILIES, COLLEAGUES, MENTORS, AND CLIENTS. YOU KNOW WHO YOU ARE. YOU ARE THE PEOPLE WHO HAVE INVESTED DEEPLY IN US AND TAUGHT US TO THINK FAR BEYOND OUR PERCEIVED LIMITATIONS.

Contents

Our Journey

· ·

Our journey for the last couple of decades has been focused on learning about the ways leaders are partnering with unlikely allies to produce new and more powerful results. We've worked with thousands of leaders—from corporations, nonprofits, and governments—and seen so much incredible work taking place when people stop leading alone. We've seen dilapidated buildings in cities transformed into bustling economic centers. We've worked with insurance companies to partner with physicians so prescriptions can be written for patients to get reimbursed for visits to parks as a source of exercise and healthy air. We've seen former felons trained to lead vibrant moving companies, earning higher income legally than they were ever able to receive in their previous illegal endeavors. We and our partners leveraged these interactions to better meet customer needs, reach new audiences for products, and develop income streams for all. This intersection where we and our partners meet, miraculously, feeds growth for our companies and for society as a whole.

However, as we progressed through our careers, we both hit a wall in understanding how to handle the complexities of leading with others. As our professional capacity grew, so too did the size and scope of our partnerships. The number and size of our stakeholders grew as well, adding complex and unfamiliar interests, diverse international cultures, and deeply layered and nuanced organizational infrastructures.

So we did what many do when they confront a challenge that requires learning and growing beyond their lived experience. In the middle of successful careers, we went back to school (that journey is likely another book in its own right). In fact, while at different times, we both got our MBAs at the UC Davis Graduate School of Management at, let's just say, ages above the mean. Thanks to our studies, we could now better recognize strategic trade-offs, assess target markets, analyze consumer needs, and build operational excellence to lower costs and increase efficiencies. And thanks to the welcoming nature of the staff, the faculty, and the international student body, we deepened our soft skills too. We learned how to recognize our innate biases, collaborate better to achieve our goals as teams, and network to build strong business relationships.

We learned so much about being better strategists, financial analysts, and marketing directors. We learned about entrepreneurship, new product development, and new business ventures. And, of course, we learned about leadership. Yet we had not been offered a single class about the successful and highly entrepreneurial ecosystem taking place where business, government, and nonprofit organizations work together synergistically. While much of what we learned may be entirely relevant to those challenges, never were the unique opportunities and possibilities at this intersection discussed. The Graduate School of Management had even started offering cutting-edge "industry immersions" during Daniel's time, which recognized that MBA and other master's and doctoral students should share a classroom to focus on the multiple players and elements that define an industry, such as agriculture or technology. But what about the *intersection* of agriculture *and* technology? Who was teaching the skills to bring together stakeholders who do not necessarily share a common vocabulary? Where were the resources for sectors trying to work together to find a common voice? And what could all of us learn from the leaders doing this work?

For Cleve, this search became an all-consuming topic. While serving as the board chair of a large foundation, Cleve enrolled in a PhD program to research the dynamics of innovation and entrepreneurship in enterprises where for-profits, nonprofits, and governments collaborate to solve pressing problems and increase profitability. He simultaneously ran Potrero Group, a consultancy that primarily serves social enterprises, and worked with entrepreneurs of all types. At UC Davis, Cleve grounded his research by gaining hands-on experience building numerous businesses from scratch that served as engines of both profitability and social change. Working with both cutting-edge academic researchers and powerful business leaders at once allowed Cleve to push and test his learnings. As it turned out, theory mattered a whole lot less than learnable skills in being able to solve real problems. The skills he identified that he saw being actively utilized by the leaders around him serve as the backbone of this book.

For Daniel, the journey went from leading nonprofit organizations to activism to expanding his business acumen by earning an MBA to finally joining Cleve at Potrero Group. At the same time, he nurtured a creative career, directing over 30 plays across the United States, performing internationally as a storyteller, and even appearing in national TV shows and commercials during a brief time in Hollywood. This combination of skills allowed him to practice innovation inside and outside the theater or set, growing the organizations he led with new strategic vision, programming, and branding, and building a voice as a social sector thought leader and convener. This eventually landed him not only the opportunity to consult with social enterprises but also opportunities to advise Fortune Global 500 companies, regional hospital systems, and local entrepreneurs in creating new products, organizational strategies, and team communication. He used this knowledge to design and curate presentations, workshops, and webinars on innovation and strategy for Cleve. Soon he became recognized as a presenter and thought leader on inter-sector collaboration himself, including winning the global U21/ PwC Innovation Challenge on the skills necessary to create jobs in a green economy.

Cleve and Daniel now bring their diverse but complementary skills to shared clients, co-presenting at conferences, co-creating case studies, and team-teaching courses and workshops. So while the skills listed in this book began as the ones identified by Cleve in his dissertation, as with many of our collaborations the boundaries of what ideas originally belonged to each of us have quickly been blurred. We also share a love of research and lifelong learning and are often most keen not to try to build something new ourselves but to share with each other and our clients exciting new theories, frameworks, and stories that we come across over the course of our days.

In essence, we've learned not to lead alone through working across our differences with each other. We've experienced the power of sharing our ideas, and learning others, in our professional life and in working together and writing this book. On that note, from the outset we'd like to be clear that few, if any, of the ideas in this book are ours alone. We've had the great fortune to work with extraordinary mentors, partners, clients, and friends. We are sponges for new ideas, yes, but we also have a knack for playing with ideas, changing them, and repurposing them in other contexts. One of Cleve's most important mentors, Professor Andy Hargadon, terms this approach "recombinant innovation." Andy has studied these phenomena for much of his career and maintains that little is new—much of what we see and experience in business is a recombination of other approaches, ideas, passions, methodologies, and so forth. Because Cleve has worked with Andy in many capacities for nearly a decade and Daniel has since studied under him as well, we can't un-ring the bell of his insights. More than any other single concept, this concept is central to our writing here and aligns to and undergirds each of our worldviews. It was both essential in our approach to our work before we met Andy and, now that we have discovered its name, prominent in a more purposeful manner since.

Many of the conclusions explored in this book are based on Cleve's in-depth study of three remarkable initiatives of leadership, innovation, and entrepreneurship done for his PhD dissertation. The first is of the Presidio Trust, an initiative to create the country's first financially self-sustaining national park, which was accomplished through unique work of the business community, the government that owns the land, and the nonprofit sector that brought remarkable flexibility and innovation to the initiative. We have included a case study on the Presidio Trust as part of this book.

The second initiative, the African Orphan Crops Consortium (AOCC), was led by Mars's chief agronomist with a focus on working to end malnutrition in Africa. While Mars is primarily known as a massive candy company, the reality is much more complicated. They're a multibillion-dollar human and pet food company, and the family and employees are deeply interested in the welfare of Africa and the people who live there. Many of the raw ingredients for Mars's products come from Africa. While not an official Mars project, the AOCC leveraged Mars's relationships and brought together a diverse group of organizations, business leaders, scientists, and government officials to do the impossible—end malnutrition.

The final initiative driving Cleve's initial research work is energy efficiency in California's residential lighting environment. Over the past 40 years, California has made progress in reducing its energy consumption, essentially keeping per capita energy usage flat over that time period, a remarkable feat given the massive proliferation of energy-consuming devices like large-screen televisions, smart devices, and computers. No other state has come close to California's progress in reducing energy use, and the reasons have everything to do with not leading alone. We have added a case study to explore this further.

In each of these examples, and the other case studies we've added in this edition, business, government, and nonprofit leaders came together in unique ways to create incredible opportunities for each partner for financial gain while also implementing large-scale collective change. We've found this to be true across industries, across decades, and, yes, across oceans. We also found the skills they used to be remarkably applicable to any business situation where you are trying to accomplish something with a colleague, collaborator, or partner who approaches work differently than you.

Our research draws from the tradition of grounded theory, which means that we bring in many, many data sources and largely qualitative sources—interviews, meeting notes, articles, lived experience—and we work to understand the big picture and draw conclusions from the work. As we noted, we will also pull from insights we've gained from over 40 combined years working as leaders ourselves at these intersections. Apropos of our topic, we'll mix and recombine these insights and approaches. We also will pull from writing and stories you might not normally find in a business book and attempt to include ideas and frameworks from across the political, cultural, and professional spectrum.

This book is the synthesis of our learnings . . . thus far. It is by its very nature incomplete. It is a snapshot of what we found on the journey at this time. We fully expect that the moment we publish it, we will find something more, different, unique that we want to add. We fully expect you to see that incompleteness and find something from your bag of tricks you think would be worth exploring too. How wonderful! We are all ears. Please share. With us or with anyone else who you think might want or need to listen. With that in mind, we've endeavored, whenever possible, to show you the original genesis of the ideas, either in the text, endnotes, or appendix at the end. While this book brings together many domains of knowledge, our hope is that you will find your way to the original sources. There is often great power in consuming an idea that feels far afield from your regular interests or focus. We have done our best so that every person who reads this book can find at least one such nugget to follow down a Google rabbit hole. We certainly did. (Are we the only ones who end up with 15 tabs open in our search engine when we look something up online?) We hope our conclusions and insights from those intellectual archeological digs are of value. Like any good archeologist, you may have different interpretations and reach different conclusions than we did. If you choose to share them, we can all continue learning from those different from ourselves.

Our collective knowledge is our collective power. Don't lead alone.

Yours,
Cleveland Justis and
Daniel Student

CHAPTER 1

Your Silo Is Burning:
Are You Ready to Put Out the Fire?

· ·

There's a funny and paradoxical thing about humanity: we have equal but opposite exponential powers to damage or create. If you look out the window, you may notice at any given time that we're juggling health crises, systemic racism, and environmental destruction that we've created through our various institutions operating comfortably in what we like to call their self-reinforcing silos. These institutions each have well-thought-out and debated theories on how to best handle these challenges and even how to be successful in the face of them. But when the problems become too much for a single institution or a single sector to control, the source of those problems is undeniable. Each sector is like a silo, an enclosed space without visibility to see how the rest of the world works. But our silos are like fishbowls in a house on fire. Things feel pretty normal and calm in the cold-water world we know, but it's about to get very, very hot.

And currently? It's quite hot. So hot that our silos are, finally, burning. And we have never been more siloed. Look to politics. Here in the United States, our two major parties, and the citizens who support them, are the very definition of self-reinforcing silos. They get their news from media organizations that speak to only their perspective, they share that perspective on the internet only with people who share their perspective, and then they cheer as their politicians, unsurprisingly, refuse to listen even a little to the other side. Countries around the world note their reluctance to trust the long-term promises of the United States. Why would they? Our presidents declare executive orders instead of passing laws, and the next person comes in and just undoes it all. When we don't allow different perspectives to challenge our preconceived notions of the world, we fail. Diseases spread because we don't trust one another. Racism perpetuates because we don't seek to understand what it's like to be in someone else's shoes. And even with our best intentions, the environment continues to get worse because we don't know how to work across our sectors effectively—because we've never had a reason to do so before!

To switch metaphors, these issues were like a boiling pot with a lid on it. Unless you picked up the lid a decade or two ago, you wouldn't see it, but it was only a matter of time before it exploded. And then *boom*. Uncontrollable wildfires, hurricanes, and tornados ravaging communities. An attempt to overthrow the government. And, of course, a multiyear pandemic. Unprepared for this symbolic and literal overflow, federal, state, and local agencies were overwhelmed, hospitals and emergency shelters overflowed, and multinational corporations and local storefronts alike overcompensated for their sudden financial and public relations crises. Now these same public, nonprofit, and private organizations need to stop trying to act alone and come together in order to find solutions.

Coming together is what it takes to address "wicked" problems.[1] Originally coined by design theorists Horst Rittel and Melvin Webber, wicked problems are unique, have no right or wrong solution, and have no clear mechanism to utilize, or no simple lever to pull, to end them. Does this sound like something your company is prepared for, even today? We guess that your answer is likely no. Does that mean your company is awful and doomed for failure? Of course not. But there is a fundamental flaw in how some companies approach their business. They ignore the opportunity to learn from their mistakes. They just keep swimming in their fishbowls assuming the world is made only of water. If wicked problems were easy to solve, they would have been solved previously. You can't just do what you always do. Wicked problems demand complex, multi-sector solutions. They are solved by seeing problems and solutions in new ways, by working with people with very different skills and approaches. And what's more, these skills and approaches not only solve wicked problems but can also raise your ability to communicate, collaborate, and get work done in nearly any situation.

Wicked problems cannot be solved by leading alone. Instead, we need to come together at what we call the "intersection." There, where our worlds collide, we can recognize how we can work together, who to work with, and how to move forward together. This is what we're going to talk about in this book.

You may feel that your organization is unprepared for the challenges of the future. Yet we are willing to bet your organization is less unprepared than it was the last time a big crisis hit. Because we *do*, in fact, learn and relearn. Slowly. Change seeps into the mainstream drip by drip, as those working in the unique niches and corners of industries start to build a movement behind new ideas. Person by person. Business by business. Sector by sector.

One possible title we explored for this book was *Entrepreneurship at the Edge*. In ecological systems, the edges of habitats are often the most productive, diverse, and important. We think the same is true in business and society. Traditionally, much of society's work has been organized into tidy sectors—businesses have focused on maximizing profits, governments provide regulation, and nonprofit organizations pick up the pieces and fill in the gaps of the social support necessary for our day-to-day lives. But the most productive, diverse, and important work in business and society often happens at the edges of these sectors.

It's there that we see businesses, nonprofits, and governments working together to establish initiatives that help solve problems they could not solve on their own. The early stages of the COVID-19 pandemic uniquely showcased the power of entrepreneurship at the edge. For a personal example, Daniel joined a short-lived, all-volunteer start-up called Hospital Hero that engineered and went live with a website in just two weeks, connecting medical service providers with volunteers who wanted to do their grocery shopping, laundry, dog walking, and more. Corporations reached out for assistance to the many projects such as this one sprouting up across the country on how to leverage items for donation, nonprofits spread the word to their networks, and politicians noted the efforts in their press conferences. There were hundreds of examples just like this. They arrived quickly. Somehow, without naming it, people across the country suddenly accessed a group of skills necessary to work together on the edges.

Society is recognizing, or re-recognizing, or probably re-re-recognizing, that solitary sectors acting as large, independent structures are too slow and clunky to be responsive to our needs. We know this doesn't have to be. We recognize that an active and adaptive government is essential to a high-performing society. And, of course, business has freedoms and financial incentives that are remarkable at generating innovation. And nonprofits often can be the most creative of all, forced by limitations to experiment with new models and ideas.

And, of course, at the edges of sectors, where the best work happens, the map doesn't end. Sectors aren't flat Earths that go from one two-dimensional end to another. They bend and overlap like bubbles. Did you know that bubbles have the least surface area for the volume that can be trapped inside them of any substance on Earth?[2] In other words, bubbles are extremely efficient at being bubbles. They would win awards for operational excellence. Except, as they touch each other, they blur form and shape, not maintaining perfect edges. When two bubbles intersect, they may lose perfection, yes, but they also become more than they were on their own. Together, they work out boundaries. They join to become bigger and that much more impressive in their new perfection than they could have been on their own.

Alone, bubbles float away. Together, they become more than the sum of their parts.

But before this metaphor floats away, let's ground it in an example. The iconic clothing company Patagonia has benefited enormously from blurring the sectors. Patagonia is one part retailer, one part social movement, and one part political dynamo. The company sees its greatest impact as a force limiting damage from climate change. Yet it dominates sales in its category of merchandise and has changed farming and procurement practices for retailers, all the while making its founder, Yvon Chouinard, a billionaire. Chouinard is also, however, a well-known environmental political campaigner, and the company's blog *The Cleanest Line* marshals and calls attention to activism and activists.[3] One percent of the sales of the company or 10 percent of the profits, whichever is larger, goes to supporting nonprofits. And in late 2022, Chouinard gave away complete ownership of Patagonia to a trust to make sure all profits address climate change. Chouinard also co-founded 1% for the Planet, which encourages other companies to do the same.[4] Their internal investment fund, Tin Shed Ventures, built up "like-minded start-ups" with seed cash.[5] The advertisements for Patagonia's brand often focus on environmental awareness first, brand second.[6] Though, of course, this *is* a way to propagate their brand. This is not just corporate social responsibility. It is corporate sales, in partnership with raising funds for public and nonprofit causes.

We look at Chouinard as a leader in his industry and applaud him. Chouinard looks back and implores us to see the Earth itself as an organizational stakeholder. And, in 2022, he famously announced just that. Indeed, a breed of innovator and entrepreneur succeeds because they know they can't do it alone. They blur the boundaries between sectors, recognizing the distinct advantages available at their intersection. Businesses are starting to maximize social returns, as well as financial returns; governments are increasingly becoming nimble; and nonprofits are blending all these approaches. But while this is uncharted territory for many, we don't have a system to teach them the skills necessary to do this work. There are no masters of inter-sector collaboration to learn to work together to solve social problems while increasing profitability. We tell the stories of people who utilize these skills with admiration for their ingenuity and impact, but we don't talk enough about the skills themselves, what they are, how they're used, and how to acquire them.

We also don't talk about how these skills can be translated to our day-to-day work, making us aware of and ready to tackle the intersections that each of us is likely to encounter, even if we don't actively collaborate outside our sector. While this book will focus on those places where the edges connect, what's great about an intersection is that you don't have to travel far (to the edge of the world, so to speak) to recognize or experience the edges. Between us, we've worked with thousands of entrepreneurs, foundation leaders, corporate leaders, nonprofit organizational leaders, and government officials collaborating under just these conditions. We've seen firsthand how this works. We believe they are necessary to you too, even if you aren't currently working between sectors. You are working with perhaps different businesses who are your suppliers or buyers, likely working with different departments, and most definitely working with different levels of seniority. Each of these is a small intersection.

While these skills are not formally learned, they are often self-taught, or perhaps peer-to-peer co-taught within unique industries where they are, quite simply, a necessity. For instance, medical professionals, public health leaders, and pharmaceutical company executives have developed strong intersection skills because their work often depends on collaborating across sectors. Likewise, real estate developers and people leading parks and protected areas, and the organizations that support them, are often particularly adept at these skills because accomplishing work on land (protecting it, developing it, and restoring it) often means that there are complicated interests across governments, nonprofits, and corporations that may be shared, or may come into conflict. These partnerships are responsible for protecting and enhancing irreplaceable natural and cultural resources with ever-shrinking financial resources. One such organization adept at this work is the Golden Gate National Parks Conservancy, which supports the national park lands surrounding San Francisco. These lands were added to the National Park Service (NPS) when the US Army no longer needed them for military purposes. Over the years, ten former military bases—including their land, thousands of buildings, and tons of garbage and toxic waste—were added to the national parks surrounding San Francisco. The government was unable to provide adequate resources to care for the massive need of the lands and buildings when the transfers came. As a result, the NPS developed entrepreneurial skills uncommon in government bodies.[7]

With the support of the nonprofit Conservancy and for-profit business ventures, the NPS changed the model of the way parks are managed. For example, they turned Alcatraz Island from a defunct prison to the area's number one tourist destination serving over 1.4 million visitors annually and with related regional economic benefits of hundreds of millions of dollars.[8] Designers from Gap helped create a museum-quality gift shop on Alcatraz—and the results spin off millions of dollars for park enhancement and protection efforts. In other parts of the park, the government and its partners transformed former military buildings into market-rate rental property and used the proceeds to support more traditional park-building activities. They helped create a stunning for-profit hotel on federal land at the base of the Golden Gate Bridge. At least five dollars of private or philanthropic investment leveraged every federal dollar invested. And yet much of this work was overseen by the same agency that manages bison in Yellowstone, the mighty Colorado River through the Grand Canyon, and the towering granite spires of Yosemite. We speak more about the unique national park partnerships in San Francisco in a case study on the Presidio Trust later in the book.

But San Francisco is far from alone in using this type of approach to revitalize our public lands. Chicago's noted Millennium Park project is owned by the city but managed and operated by a nonprofit. Friends of the High Line in New York City, a nonprofit, are instrumental in raising the funds for the city's greening of its former aboveground subway tracks. In San Jose, some for-profit private developers are planning a $150 million art and cultural installation that will likely transform an aging city park into a transformed gem in the heart of Silicon Valley.[9]

Yet these approaches demonstrated in the environmental sector are far from common. Necessity is the mother of invention, surely, and for many other sectors there is simply no clear need to work outside their silo. Without necessity, we tend to fall into a loop where the lessons we learn about how to do work are recycled and regurgitated back. This is why we call these types of silos "self-reinforcing." The world we see is the world we know, and we become convinced, falsely, that it is just the way the whole world works.

 DETOUR: Shared value in practice

As we move through this book, we will share a few ideas that are related, but not central, to our main point. On the road to the intersection of businesses, governments, and nonprofits, these concepts might be worth the scenic view. They will add to the overall richness of your understanding of our central concepts but are not critical or directly connected to our narrative. Once you finish reading, just merge back onto the main road and rejoin us!

A core skill any business school teaches is competitive strategy—how to position your company to beat the competitors. Mr. Competitive Strategy is Harvard Business School's Michael Porter, who established the theory of Five Forces way back in 1979.[10] In gauging the attractiveness of entering or shifting in an industry to gain competitive advantage, he argued businesses needed to recognize the possible threat of New Entrants (Netflix . . . say bye-bye, Blockbuster) and Substitutes (why take a train when you can fly there?), the relative power of Buyers (the people/business spending money on your product) and Suppliers (the company you are spending money on to make your product), and as the central tenet, the intensity of rivalry from Competitors (Pepsi vs. Coke, the cola wars).

Of course, this framing of strategy was built on the idea of first deciding which industry, or silo, your business should compete in. And that made sense. If you were McDonald's, it would be much more productive to focus on how to compete for customers with Burger King than with Nike.

But in 2011, Porter introduced a new theory with Mark Kramer that recognized that part of strategy was not competition, but to "create shared value" in the intersections between the institutions that serve society.[11] Creating shared value, Porter and Kramer noted, differentiated itself because it saw social good as a business model. For decades, to legitimize their operations and the toll they would take on society, corporations balanced, as best they could, the income they generated from the citizenry by incurring costs to invest in a charitable cause. These corporate social responsibility initiatives have generated some important work, but many have become little more than public relations machines. So instead of choosing a cause that the CEO cared about—or worse, simply looked the best—Porter and Kramer argued that a better strategy would be to choose an agenda specific to the company's ability to grow its product. After all, integral to having a competitive strategy is developing the capacity of a workforce and the buying power of the consumer. Why would you treat this part of your business any different? If you invest in growing a community to provide more skilled labor and reach higher spending power, you will do better for yourself and better for others. Which perhaps means that building up a system that serves everyone's needs can be as powerful as, if not more powerful than, simply winning at another's expense.

The idea becomes even more provocative if you think of shared value not just with labor and consumers but actually with other businesses and other sectors as well. Geoff Kendall, cofounder and CEO of the Future-Fit

continued

Foundation, labeled three themes his team saw in sustainability reports businesses were issuing in response to the United Nation's 2030 Sustainable Development Goals.[12] The first was a "defensive" theme, noting new jobs created and emissions reduced that limit costly environmental fees. The second, tied to Porter and Kramer's "shared value," was a "selective" theme that noted actions that impacted specific shared societal goals.

The third, a "holistic" theme, saw businesses transform their practices to make choices to solve challenges shared across societal institutions. They didn't just act to reduce poverty, but they also built greater food resources while doing so, elevating social entrepreneurs who produced local products that drove down their bottom line, helping local nonprofits and governments avoid costly shipping fees. This is what happens when you don't lead alone. And "by looking at all interactions between the company and its suppliers, its customers, other socioeconomic actors, and the environment," Kendall writes, "it is possible to identify otherwise unforeseen issues."[13] Beating the competition is great, but building the resilience to survive when the competitive forces turn against you can be even more critical. This is how you arm yourself to be resilient in the face of those wicked problems. And it is folly to think they aren't coming.

Indeed, put together Kendall's theory of value and Porter's widely accepted idea of strategy, and what you have is an interesting potential truth. Short-term success may come from pulling the five-force lever, but long-term success for any business—corporate, nonprofit, or public—must be achieved by recognizing and participating in the larger systems, networks, and movements in which they operate.

So what do you do in a time where governments, corporations, and nonprofits are watching their silos burning down? Use it as an excuse to stop pretending that they operate in different spheres in the first place! Indeed the solution is, and has always been, actually quite simple. As we frequently tell our clients, "uncomfortable does not have to mean unnavigable." To further our intersection metaphor, there is a map to this work and there is even a route we recommend you follow. But you, and you alone, have to walk it. That's where it gets complex. That's where you have choices. We will seek to recombine ideas, theories, and real-life practices we've learned from others with the skills that have emerged from our own experiences that are necessary for this work. But then you have to actually do the work, even if it doesn't feel immediately necessary. And that takes a brave first step. Think of it as a red pill/blue pill scenario from *The Matrix*. Are you ready to actually see the truth? Are you ready to no longer lead alone? Are you ready to be united with the innovators and entrepreneurs who have been working for generations at the intersection? Or, even simpler, are you ready to think about the work you do today in a new way, with new possibilities?

To greater challenges, we *collectively* bring better solutions. That, we'd like to believe, is our collective story. So what, specifically, do you need to learn to be a leader at this intersection, ready to merge onto the open road of shared success? This is the focus of the remainder of the book. Thanks for joining us on the journey.

CHAPTER 2

The Skills You'll Need to Bring with You

. . . .

Let's begin, as many literal journeys to an intersection begin, by just getting in the car. We assume that you already have lots of skills and that you've picked up this book to help grow yourself as a leader working at the intersection of sectors. What would you want to bring besides this book to take to the intersection? We suggest you pack leadership, change management, and domain-specific skills with you on this journey. Many books and articles are dedicated to and go deep in each of these categories, so here we'll just show you why they're important. Having strong capacity in these three areas will provide an important backbone to the complex skills, many of which borrow from these core groups of skills, that you will need to utilize to work at the intersection.

Leadership skills

To learn to not lead alone, you first must simply learn to lead. Organizations have many types of leaders, even if the leaders aren't officially in a leadership role. Some leadership skills are specific to very unique situations, such as the intersection work we will detail in this book. But some leadership skills . . . you just need them to drive. Many of these principles are time-tested and are widely considered foundational to leading (or working) in any sector. So while there are specific needs for each, the same skills are used by corporate leaders in many of our leading companies, bureaucrats building governmental programs, and nonprofits serving communities. The literature on core leadership skills is large, and we encourage you to dive in. Many of our favorites are in the appendix. For the purposes of this book, however, we are going to get specific to leadership that is uniquely important to working with people with whom we may have no innate comfort or familiarity. This will be interwoven through nearly everything we introduce.

Change management skills

When you're first learning to drive, you're almost entirely focused on learning the rules of the road. Yet once you actually hit the road, you have to adapt what you know to meet the unique challenges of the moment, gaining a more nuanced understanding of the behavior of people in the other cars. Managing a company as it changes requires those same skills. When you require people to modify their values and their approaches in this manner, it takes a specific kind of leadership known more broadly as change management.

One of our favorite change management theorists is the godfather of adaptive leadership, Dr. Ronald Heifetz. He pointed out that leaders often tackled technical challenges that were easy to identify and lent themselves to quick and easy solutions that were accepted by all stakeholders. He also warned, however, that technical solutions were frequently misidentified when, in actuality, they were what he called adaptive challenges.

The risk in having deep technical knowledge is that it can keep an individual more embedded in the status quo. Corporate hiring practices are infected with this reality. The danger in a company's growth is com-placency sets in and the original experimental culture that allowed them to outflank the competition is diminished or lost. To compensate, companies put a lot of effort into finding innovative thinkers willing to challenge the status quo. Yet, all too often, the same people tasked with hiring unconventional candidates are also tasked with hiring candidates with specialized certifications and technical skill sets that ultimately must come first. After all, units have financial benchmarks they have to reach, and the work needs to get done. So companies end up hiring the known and then sacrifice innovation.

We will venture into adaptive leadership, certainly, as well as other forms of change management. We are, however, pun intended, adapt-ing them for our purposes. Lucky for you, we've done a deep dive into change management practices for our own clients, and we've shared a number of these resources in the appendix.

Domain-specific skills

Domain-specific skills are often the first thing learned in a professional setting, and logically so, as they are typically developed for specific tasks. First and foremost, domain-specific skills allow you to get very specific work accomplished and to get inside the system you're seeking to change. For example, it is hard to work in the banking system if you don't know the basics of finance and business. It is nearly impossible to work in the medical field without specific medical training. Domain-specific skills allow you the core knowledge and authority to maneuver and make change in that field.

Domain-specific skills are equally important at the intersections of your field and will be extremely useful in each of the buckets of skills we will present in this book. To start, if you want to work at an intersection and you don't have skills and experience in the systems that make up that intersection, you'll need to spend time acquiring those skills until you are able to think like a system and understand the approaches, skills, and language at play. We're not saying you need to become an engineer, scientist, or technician, but we are recommending that you invest time and energy to be able to project confidence and ask good questions.

Additionally, one of the most powerful aspects of domain-specific skills is that by having them and employing them, you'll know the right type of people to bring into the initiative to meet your goals. As we will argue in this book, most successful initiatives at the intersection of sectors are created by acting like a network and bringing people with diverse skills together who can contribute to the work. These skills also then give you legitimacy with others who may hold the power and are setting the parameters of the conversation. Sometimes it is critical to maintain at least symbolic conformity to the dominant paradigm. To be taken seriously as a change-maker, you must be seen as credible, smart, relevant, and knowledgeable.

You also want domain-specific skills to help shift approaches and debates as you employ our final set of skills, *Lead Like a Movement*. Technical information is often not easily understood by nonexperts. Domain-specific skills allow a leader to have credibility and change the conversation. In other words, you can't learn to do something stronger or better until you first learn to do it right.

Applying your skills to more complex situations

You must practice all these core skills to be successful in any situation that requires diverse stakeholders. Again, like learning to drive, put yourself in simple situations first—with your team at work, with your family, within your social media interactions. As you progress, think about other ways of putting these skills to the test, such as at conferences and networking events and cross-departmental meetings. Think of it as starting to interact with regular traffic and changing lanes before interacting with pedestrians, four-way stops, and left-turn lanes.

This book, on the other hand, is all about those more complex scenarios—the intersections. Ultimately, you don't become a good driver because of driving school. The real manual comes from being out there, interacting with traffic. And much as you realize after spending some time on the road that many drivers' skills are underdeveloped, we have become convinced after studying and working with thousands of leaders that intersection skills are also underdeveloped in most people. Our schooling and training taught us to lead from just the view out of our own car window, our personal and professional silo. We aim to get really good at doing the thing we do and then inspire others around us by being so good at it. This makes sense—unless you're trying to accomplish important work with people with very different goals, motivations, organizations, and life experiences than your own.

The good news? Skills can be learned, developed, and refined over time. This comes in sharp contrast to the "hero worship" many of us learn about great leaders. We learn about societal change-makers, whether it be Martin Luther King Jr. or Steve Jobs, and they become larger than life. Yet rarely do we learn about the skills they utilized in their work that made them truly extraordinary. The qualities they have that are not just intrinsic.

This book is organized around three overarching themes: *Think Like a System*, *Act Like a Network*, and *Lead Like a Movement*. Each of these themes has a series of skills grouped under that theme. How did Martin Luther King Jr., for instance, figure out that nonviolence would be such an effective tool to change people's perspectives? We would argue that he utilized *Think Like a System* skills to understand how the system worked and his role in it. How did he recruit such a diverse group of stakeholders to march alongside him? We would argue that he utilized *Act Like a Network* skills to connect his movement with others and find new collaborators. And last, but certainly not least, how did he unite them to hold one another's hands and walk straight into harm's way? We would argue that he utilized *Lead Like a Movement* skills to bring different sections of society together and point them in a unified direction.

We don't want to tell you about great leaders. We want to tell you about what these great leaders did (i.e., the skills they utilized) that allowed them to be great. You don't need to be them—but you can see why they succeeded and how you can too.

CHAPTER 3

The Skills You'll Acquire

. . . .

We've spent a lot of time working with and studying leaders at inter-sections. Some were profoundly successful, many were profoundly unsuccessful, and most were somewhere in the middle. Common among all of them was a specific set of skills that were sometimes consciously used and other times not. As we worked to better understand these skills, we noticed that they fell into three relatively tidy groups. While "Think Like a System, Act Like a Network, and Lead Like a Movement" is a pithy slogan, it also helped us better understand what we were seeing and evolved into this book. Throughout the book, we'll share the skills, robust real-life examples, and exercises designed to help you develop your capacity to use them yourself.

The book is divided into three sections, with each chapter covering a particular skill. In each section we also explore at least one case study that encompasses a number of the skills discussed in that section.

THINK LIKE A SYSTEM
Understand your desired impact and how it fits into a larger picture

- Observing with curiosity
- Recognizing patterns and trends
- Taking a big step back
- Listening with empathy and reflection
- Tapping into intuition
- Reframing for a new way of seeing things

ACT LIKE A NETWORK
Connect your work to others and find new collaborators

- Acting as a part of a whole
- Getting out of your silo
- Learning other professional languages
- Code-mixing with intention
- Understanding hidden power
- Rewarding risk

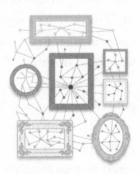

LEAD LIKE A MOVEMENT
Bring collaborators together and move them in a unified direction

- Building diversity
- Integrating multiple logics
- Establishing feedback loops
- Saying no
- Managing dissonance
- Managing incumbents
- Managing secret agendas

Think like a system:
Understand your desired impact and how it fits into a larger picture

Thinking like a system means changing our thinking from how we as individuals have an impact to how a larger community can have an impact (and what our role within that community is). This shift helps us to harness resources outside our own domain and has greater impact with less work—we get the full power of the system and its leverage to help us.

Much has been written about systems thinking in organizations. Peter Senge popularized these ideas, particularly in his much-revered book, *The Fifth Discipline*. According to Senge, the core of systems thinking "is to understand how it is that the problems that we all deal with, which are the most vexing, difficult, and intransigent, come about, and to give us some perspective on those problems [in order to] give us some leverage and insight as to what we might do differently."[1]

Senge and many other systems thinkers help leaders see that all organizations are complex, constantly changing systems, and that they're dependent on many other interdependent systems. Additionally, systems thinkers encourage us to build learning into all we do to foster growth, flexibility, and the ability to manage change. Finally, they challenge us to always be alert to the world around us, scanning for relationships between seemingly disparate parts of our lives.

But what do we mean by "system"? A good example that Senge mentions is families. We are individuals, and we are usually part of a larger family system with its own unique collective history and patterns of interactions that might seem quite normal to us but completely foreign to someone else. In a work setting, when we are faced with a challenge, we utilize systems thinking to look beyond our own skills, to think about the whole system in which we're embedded—our team, our organization, our industry, and our partners. By looking at the whole system, we can see challenges, opportunities, and solutions that were impossible when looking at the situation through a smaller framework.

We've identified six skills that are particularly important to developing competence and proficiency in thinking like a system:

- Observing with curiosity
- Recognizing patterns and trends
- Taking a big step back
- Listening with empathy and reflection
- Tapping into intuition
- Reframing for a new way of seeing things

The next section of this book will dive deeply into each of these skills and help you find ways to develop your proficiency with them. A few people have refined these skills to accurately see otherwise hidden signals of change, like entrepreneurs who build companies that seem to solve problems we didn't even know we had. But even at their most basic application, these skills can produce profound results. Kenneth Mikkelsen and Harold Jarche published an article some years ago in the *Harvard Business Review* that illustrated why the skills developed in thinking like a system are so important for building great organizations and avoiding powerful problems.[2] The article shares a story about race car driver Juan Manuel Fangio in the 1950 Monaco Grand Prix, when he hit the brakes as he went screeching around a turn, just in time to avoid crashing into a multicar accident. An act of inspired luck? Pure athletic genius? Or using systems thinking?

Fangio had studied a photograph of a similar accident in a previous race at this very spot. He had noticed how the turned heads of fans in the stands gave a darker hue than one might expect in that area of the photograph. He saw the same dark color as he approached the turn and saved quite possibly not only his own life that day.

Mikkelsen and Jarche use this story to point out how leaders must "scan the world for signals of change,"[3] but we see something much simpler in this tale: leaders, innovators, inventors, and others like them look around at what others are doing. Like a point guard in basketball, they are always scanning the environment for change. In observing how things are playing out in front of us, we start noticing how our world works—how the players on our teams or the fans in the stands are existing in relation to ourselves. In short, we are beginning to think like a system. Our success lies in our understanding of the relationships between everything we are seeing.

But, of course, simply *thinking* in a way that makes sense of our interrelated world is not enough. We will still be alone, dreaming of companionship. This leads us to our second set of skills, *Act Like a Network*.

Act like a network:
Connect your work to others and find new collaborators

Acting like a network allows you and the initiative you're working on to greatly magnify your impact and innovation. Networks have a remarkable ability to accomplish work efficiently because you're not trying to do everything all on your own. In fact, if you're tapping into networks, you're likely finding people who are much better at some of the work than you are. Perhaps more importantly, when you tap into networks, you're tapping into areas of knowledge you didn't know existed. You're learning what you didn't know you didn't know. This is why so many great companies and organizations take a network-based approach: it helps them uncover their blind spots and work in new ways. To be clear, we're not talking about connecting with others to promote yourself or your company. We're talking about acting like a computer network, a neural network—or a network of very different people and organizations.

To act like a network, you'll need to develop competence in the following areas:

- Acting as a part of a whole

- Getting out of your silo

- Learning other professional languages

- Code-mixing with intention

- Understanding hidden power

- Rewarding risk

These skills get you out of your own intellectual, organizational, and conceptual silos. There's so much you can learn, adapt, and harness from other people, perspectives, and organizations. When you act like a network, you're using not just your own skills and knowledge but also others' for results that far exceed what you can do on your own. John Kania and Mark Kramer, whom we referenced in our detour in the first chapter, generated a concept called "collective impact" that acts as good source material for this concept. They argued that the nonprofit sector, in particular (but we would argue you could extrapolate this out to any sector, really), "most frequently operates using an approach that we call isolated impact. It is an approach oriented toward finding and funding a solution embodied within a single organization, combined with the hope that the most effective organizations will grow or replicate to extend their impact more widely."[4]

Acting like a network sets you up to do more than just hope that someone will notice what you are doing. You bring a parade of potential partners into your sphere. And since you are already thinking like a system, you become a learning machine from all these new influences. Indeed, once you start looking at how other people perceive the world, you can start adopting their best practices. Are you planning on being a race car driver like Fangio anytime soon? Probably not. Might you easily find yourself remembering this practice in another scenario, noticing how a crowd is looking at something to anticipate a situation? Definitely!

In the aptly titled *Cracking the Network Code: Four Principles for Grantmakers*, written by Jane Wei-Skillern, Nora Silver, and Eric Heitz, the authors deliver ideas on how organizations can work together within and outside their sector to build their impact.[5] Principle four is to be a "node, not hub," which means to see yourself as one part of a larger web of activity, not a central station. "'Node thinking' succeeds because resources of all types—leadership, money, talent—have dramatically more impact when leveraged across organizations, fields, and sectors." This is, in essence, sharing the wealth to the greater benefit of all. You are bringing your work into something much larger. If you bring the best of what you have and I bring the best of what I have, surely what we have together is better than what either of us has individually. To accomplish this as effectively as possible, the authors suggest getting "multiple boats in the water." In other words, success is about how many different boats can make up your fleet, not about being the biggest boat in the fleet.

It might seem like race car drivers like Fangio, or famous tennis players or golfers, or CEOs, or presidents, or movie stars, accomplish what they do by being the biggest, most important boats in the water. And they certainly do have leadership skills and technical skills that magnify their impact. But time and time again, when you take a closer look, the best and the brightest are backed by the best teams, institutions, and partnerships.

As Kania and Kramer argue, however, "collaboration is nothing new. The social sector is filled with examples of partnerships, networks, and other types of joint efforts. . . . Unlike most collaborations, collective impact initiatives involve a centralized infrastructure, a dedicated staff, and a structured process that leads to a common agenda, shared measurement, continuous communication, and mutually reinforcing activities among all participants."[6]

We couldn't agree more. This leads us to our final set of skills, *Lead Like a Movement*.

Lead like a movement:
Bring collaborators together and point them in a unified direction

Movements allow us to think greater and change our relationship with the world. We often think of social movements in terms of activists and politics, but many successful companies have built social movements into their work. IKEA built a social movement to make highly designed, fashionable Euro-chic furniture affordable for everyone. Companies like Apple ("Think Different") or Volkswagen ("Drivers Wanted") build entire marketing campaigns around the movement of people you can join by buying their products.

Governments, too, utilize social movement approaches in their work, particularly in public health campaigns, such as stopping smoking and reducing vaping behavior. Traditionally, governments try to change citizens' behaviors through laws and regulations. In social movement approaches, a government aims to galvanize large numbers of people into acting in an organized way and motivating people to take political actions. In these cases, the government becomes the catalyst, and their work becomes so much more powerful.

Leading like a movement is where you'll seriously heighten the impact of the system you've come to understand, leverage the network you've gathered, and harness powerful forces to use for change. You're tapping into people's deeper needs and desires for creating a better world—even if it's hard. Think Mahatma Gandhi, Nelson Mandela, or Greta Thunberg. They brought diverse groups of people together to accomplish the impossible. But they weren't, at least initially, elected to be leaders. They weren't handed authority, and others weren't told to follow them. They just helped others around them understand the flow of the traffic of their movement and helped them see their role in it. Over time and through their attention to aligning a network of people to move together in a single direction, people turned to them to lead.

You don't have to be Gandhi to create change. And change can happen at the intersection of an entire country's political and social system, but it can also happen at your weekly company meeting. Either way, learning to lead others in new ways can be challenging. Minimum viable consortia (MVC) is a newer model of collaboration recently advanced by a group of researchers called the Stakeholder Alignment Collaborative. Building on agile methodologies in entrepreneurship, the MVC approach aims to simplify collaboration by not overplanning it. The model encourages collaborations to (1) align their interests, (2) act together and separately, and (3) adjust the collaboration by reviewing progress, resolving disputes, and celebrating success. We aim to keep things similarly simple for you.[7]

A better world is just that—something improved from where it was before because we've built out a process to fix it. We seek this in our own lives in small ways, with our small victories solving our day-to-day problems. By observing these leaders, you can see the impact we can have when we bring stakeholders from diverse backgrounds to an intersection to solve something quite huge.

We've worked with and studied movement leaders and have distilled the skills they utilize to the following:

- **Building diversity**
- **Integrating multiple logics**
- **Establishing feedback loops**
- **Saying no**
- **Managing dissonance**
- **Managing incumbents**
- **Managing secret agendas**

Acquiring these skills and using them in your work with other sectors will magnify your impact. Mathematician and philosopher Antanas Mockus, mayor of Bogotá, Columbia, from 1995 to 1997 and again from 2001 to 2003, is a great example of a movement leader. His movement?

Ending traffic fatalities. When Mockus first took office, over 1,300 people died each year in Bogotá in traffic accidents.[8] When he arrived in office, he inherited a 1991 constitutional reform strengthening the mayor's ability to work within the confines of national laws and regulations. Mockus then issued 350,000 thumbs-up/thumbs-down placards to the public to call out the dangerous behavior of their fellow citizens. The city traffic police department was abolished, and traffic safety became the responsibility of the general metropolitan force. Starting with Mockus and continuing with other mayors, bike and bus lanes were built. The problem was tackled from all angles, each sector with its own agendas. Mockus couldn't just tell them what to do if he wanted sustainable results. In fact, democracies as a political system are built to keep leaders from establishing lasting agendas without buy-in from the people. They sustain only if the leaders can deftly maneuver behind closed doors and build a groundswell for the work. And the groundswell is ongoing. In 2017, the city announced a "Vision Zero" road safety plan—a day in which the number of road fatalities in Bogotá is zero.[9]

Yes, Mockus was the mayor, but he was certainly far from a political insider and the problem he wanted to solve was far more than one office could achieve. He played one critical role that he earned as much as he was given: he took all those great teams, institutions, and sectors and deftly pointed them in a unified direction.

You can too.

PART 1

THINK LIKE A SYSTEM

CHAPTER 4

Think Like a System Overview

. . . .

As we discussed in chapter 3, much has been written about systems thinking in organizations. It would be foolhardy and redundant to rehash all this great thinking and writing. Our goal in this part of the book is to attune you to the skills that our research and experience have shown to be essential in systems thinking when working at the intersection of business, government, and nonprofit sectors.

The origin of systems thinking is usually traced to Ludwig von Bertalanffy, who in the 1950s moved the field of organization study toward the idea that organizations act like networks of people, procedures, technologies, and activities.[1] This approach came in stark contrast to the prevailing wisdom at the time that saw organizations more as machines than integrated open systems.

At the core of systems thinking is the idea that in order to create change or form robust partnerships, we need to understand the broader system in which we and our partners operate. We intentionally named this part of the book *Think Like a System* because we wanted to emphasize the importance of thinking and understanding *before* acting (the next part of the book). As Peter Senge and many other systems scholars remind us, organizations are part of complex interdependent systems. Thus, systems approaches can have enormous positive benefits or powerful disastrous results. Collaboration introduces complexity and the need for intense focus on the partnership in addition to the work being accomplished by each partner. Before creating partnerships, we need to spend time and focused attention on learning and thinking about who we are and how we fit.

Noted systems scholars Christian Seelos and Johanna Mair undertook an extensive study of systems change initiatives and found that most fall into one of two broad categories:[2] (1) the initiatives didn't work to transform an existing system but instead tried to move the system to a new, perhaps more innovative and effective trajectory, or (2) the initiatives worked intensely on individual subsystems in order to transform the system at large. To us, both of these categories point to a universal truth; you have to work to understand your system before you can tackle its change or look to the larger systems it is part of. Seelos and Mair further emphasized the importance of careful study of systems before intervening in them. We second this importance.

To that end, we've identified six skills that are particularly important to developing competence and proficiency in thinking like a system in initiatives at the intersection of sectors:

- **Observing with curiosity**
- **Recognizing patterns and trends**
- **Taking a big step back**
- **Listening with empathy and reflection**
- **Tapping into intuition**
- **Reframing for a new way of seeing things**

These skills each have their own chapter in this section so that you can better understand and begin to practice the skills.

Curious as to how we do that? Well, that's an appropriate feeling to have!

CHAPTER 5

Observing with Curiosity

· ·

Dr. Francesca Gino argues that "most of the breakthrough discoveries and remarkable inventions throughout history, from flints for starting a fire to self-driving cars, have something in common: they are the result of curiosity."[1] As objective evidence, Gino notes a study conducted by Spencer Harrison, a professor at the internationally famous business school INSEAD. In a survey Harrison led, a one-unit increase in curiosity (measured in numerical self-ratings) was associated with 34 percent more products created and made available over a two-week period from artists on an e-commerce website. In a more formal work environment, Gino conducted her own research, sending text messages at the beginning of the workday to two groups of employees. For one group, she asked what they were curious about; for the other group, she asked what they would engage in that day. After a month of texts, Gino surveyed both groups and discovered that the first group demonstrated far more innovative behaviors in the workplace.

This is an important finding because in our society, although we might start as a curious child, as we move through childhood and into adulthood, we begin a long cycle of being rewarded not for the good questions we have but for the answers we can provide. If you ever had to shoot your hand in the air to be rewarded for knowing something in a classroom, you've experienced this reward.

Yet in intersection work, our goal is not to seek answers; it's to seek better questions. This helps us see and better understand the system we're trying to influence. Yet this goes against what we've been socialized for since our earliest days. We often are taught to focus, know the answer, move forward, and keep being productive. But to begin to think like a system, we need to teach ourselves to be curious about it in the first place.

In an *HBR IdeaCast* podcast about her article, Gino tells a story about how she now encourages, rather than shuts down, her children.[2] When she finds them at 6 a.m. in the kitchen opening cabinets and making a mess, instead of scolding and cleaning, she now joins in. She prompts them with queries to encourage them to think about the system they are curiously exploring. She no longer worries that they will make a mess. In fact, she says that "things don't end up in a mess—most of the time." Even when it does, the entertainment she gets from their exploration is worth more to her.

The host, Curt Nickisch, replies that the only downside really is that "you [just] have to be willing to clean up the salt." That's not that hard! Words to live by!

Gino has seen organizations benefit from encouraging curiosity, as well. She tells Nickisch, "It's pretty clear to people when it is that it's time to ask questions, to really wonder, to explore and when it's time to put our heads down and just execute on the work." The key is to create an environment that rewards curiosity instead of punishing it. This becomes even more important when you are dealing with the complicated factors at intersections. To succeed when tasks become more complex, we want to re-engage our childhood curiosity. Some people might equate curiosity with distraction, but a healthy amount of curiosity and observation allows us to move forward with smart decisions.

"Be clear on when and how curiosity is valued. And also making sure that if people explore, the explorations are intelligent ones," Gino says. So what does intelligent exploration look like? In intersection work, we want to expand our attention, looking at the entire environment, especially those things that don't seem related. In a sense, you want to find your perspective and notice what you might be missing from where you stand. You want to see how you are seeing the world and recognize how others, depending on where they are, might see it differently. Toddlers, or a fish in a fishbowl, can be curious only from a "me"-centric perspective. As we evolve into adults, our intelligence comes in knowing that this may not be the only reality.

To extend our ongoing metaphor, if your car was your silo, what might you see out of that car window? Perhaps an interesting building with a unique design. You might wonder how someone came up with that. Soon you find yourself asking, "How might the changes in that design apply to the product I am trying to redesign?" Or perhaps you are on a country road and pass a group of cows in a field. You are struck that one of them is far in the corner compared to the others. You wonder why the cow did that. Soon you find yourself asking, "What in my life might be worth being a little bit more alone in my opinion on?" With that in mind, we recommend a practice of observation that is simple but requires a certain amount of bravery to undertake it.

 Practicing observing with curiosity

Before jumping into a work situation, especially an intersection situation, take the time to simply observe. First, pay attention to your thoughts. To train yourself to observe your own thoughts, spend your first minute or two simply writing them down. This works great in larger gatherings and virtual spaces. Online, you could even keep your camera off for an extra minute or two, a totally socially acceptable option to just observe. Just as in the examples we provided on looking out your car window, allow yourself to wonder why people behave the way that they do or make certain common or uncommon choices. This can have a dual purpose. Write down

continued

questions you have about yourself in relation to those choices—what might happen if you did that or what does that mean about you? Then also think about them. What does that mean about them? As a side bonus, you might find that this practice becomes a conversation starter. You can share that your habit bolsters your focus and desire to find perspective so that you can better lead innovative entrepreneurial efforts. That tiny action of curiosity, once shared, will have unbridled power.

The goal is to just be really curious about everyone and everything around you. Often we're so busy focusing on what we want to say or accomplish that we forget to be open to all of the lessons from those whom we're interacting with regularly. With so many different voices and life experiences, there is much to be curious about.

CHAPTER 6

Recognizing Patterns and Trends

. . . .

Once you've collected a host of new observations about your environment, it's time to process that information. The key to changing how you shift to thinking like a system is to recognize patterns and trends. The ability to recognize patterns and trends, however, often comes from experience, creating a bit of a conundrum. Every intersection is different. You need to give yourself the space to make mistakes.

To return to our well-trodden metaphor, Harold Smith, who founded the first professional driving training company in the United States in 1952, often referred to what he called the "space cushion"[1]—the space between your car and other cars to give you space to comfortably take your eye off what's right ahead of you in order to look around. Creating space in intersection work gives you time to look around and to err in your judgment as you get acquainted with the systems that compose the intersection in which you're working. It's inevitable: you *will* make mistakes as you learn. That's part of being human. This work is too important, and the stakes are too high not to give yourself a space cushion for learning.

In their previously referenced article, "Mastering System Change," Christian Seelos and Johanna Mair write that you have to "do things right before doing the right thing. . . . The goal for systems change apprentices is to make small, safe steps and to learn how to walk before picking up momentum and starting to run. Perhaps it's best if we swallow our pride, ambition, and beliefs in our own competence. Instead, let's do something simple first, learn a lot about a target system, and re-engage with our mission later."[2]

Recognition usually comes from closely observing ourselves and the world around us, with repeated exposure to one thing or exposure to many things deepening our experience. Yet many of us have failed to do this well. We don't know what has made us successful, why we've failed at tasks, and what conditions have contributed to these successes and failures. Since we've buried our childhood curiosity of looking out the car window and focused only on driving the road ahead, we haven't really given ourselves the time or space to explore. This is why many of us see therapists! When we recognize our own patterns, we can learn how to shape a different future.

Data scientists are investing huge amounts of time and money into using machine learning algorithms to detect characteristics and categories within data, yet our brains have some of the best pattern recognition systems available. Ray Kurzweil was one of the pioneers of pattern recognition technology in computers and artificial intelligence. *Forbes* called him the "ultimate thinking machine" and rightfully so. He would be the first to tell you that everything we train our machines to do is all modeled from what goes on in the human brain. So when Kurzweil built the first "reading machine" for blind people, he broke it down so that it recognized words like the human brain did. First individual letters, then words, then groups of words, and so forth.[3]

Noted astrophysicist Neil deGrasse Tyson explains our highly evolved ability to recognize patterns as "over centuries of evolution, humans' pattern recognition skills determined natural selection. Hunters skilled at spotting prey and predator and telling poisonous plants from healthy ones offered them a better chance of survival than those blind to the patterns. It enabled the survivors to pass on those pattern-friendly genes to future generations."[4]

It is perhaps of no surprise then that leaders and innovators are frequently self-described lifelong learners. By seeking out new experiences, they not only collect new observations but also see connections among them. In his book *Always Day One*, Silicon Valley journalist Alex Kantrowitz interviews 130 employees and leaders of big tech companies. Through these interviews, he discovers what he calls a "day one mindset," in which companies like Amazon, Apple, and Meta (Facebook) treat every day like it's their first. "They attack new markets without worrying about their flagship businesses. They are in a constant mode of reinvention," Kantrowitz says.[5] Without a day one mindset, Amazon might still be an online bookstore. Apple would still be known for its computers instead of its iPhones. Day two, says Jeff Bezos, is "stasis, followed by irrelevance, followed by excruciating, painful decline, followed by death."[6]

Of course, this is not something that just happens circumstantially in these innovative companies. Employees are encouraged to be curious. They can think about the entire system rather than getting lost in the everyday details. These companies also focus on automating simpler tasks as they grow, allowing even lower-level employees to not only worry about the nuts and bolts of their direct work but also think about and share new ideas. As a result, many employees have the same freedom to imagine possibilities every day as they did when the company was just a small, nimble business without massive expectations to meet. Their employees can look up and scan the horizon. Google, for instance, had what's known as "20% time." Since their early days, employees have been urged to spend one-fifth of their time on their own projects, outside their regular work, that they think will benefit Google.[7] Back in the day, Gmail was reportedly born from this. But a decade later, in a much larger company, so was Google Cardboard.[8]

Most of us aren't blessed with work environments that find a way to keep a day one mentality. So just like you need to find time for the gym to stay in shape when your job doesn't do it for you, the best way to notice patterns and trends is to build diversity into your life outside work. As we like to say at our consulting firm, Potrero Group, "you don't know what you don't know." It's up to you to find the time to find out what that is.

 Practicing recognizing patterns and trends

If the only way to build your pattern recognition skills is to explore new-to-you ideas, then why not have fun exploring those ideas? Start by brainstorming ten topics or activities you're curious about but have never truly explored. Enter one of these curiosities into a search engine to find simple, time-reduced ways to explore it. You might read a free beginner's guide, take a one-off virtual class, listen to a podcast, or watch a series of short videos. Let's call this your "not-work" list.

Let your curiosity lead you! For example, to explore his own passions, Daniel has taken a curling class at the local ice-skating rink, has taken an online crepe-making class on Airbnb, has listened to podcast episodes about people in different careers approaching their work, and regularly watches what his wife affectionately calls "YouTube University"—how-to videos from everything from home plant care to car maintenance. Think about the patterns at play during, but most importantly after, the experience. If possible, keep a journal about it and free-associate. This is a method of psychology that dates to none other than Sigmund Freud. We don't immediately analyze or censor what we think; we simply allow ourselves to explore. What's interesting to you?

It's interesting that in curling, one person calls out instructions to two others on whether or not to sweep the ice in front of the "stone" to make it smooth for it to keep sliding along (watch the Winter Olympics to see what we mean). It's interesting that in making crepes, all the ingredients are warmed in a single pan, together. In both instances, "ingredients" work together only because one person carefully monitors their interactions. Try reviewing your journal after each experience and look back at your prior free associations. You will find yourself recognizing more and more overlapping patterns.

This won't be a quick skill to pick up, as it requires short bursts of immersion in lots of topics. The payoff will come in moments when you least expect it—when you are sitting at work trying to solve a problem, and suddenly, you are thinking about curling (we swear, it's a fun sport!). Once you've built diversity into your personal life, you will instinctively start finding relationships with everything. This is really the only way to know you've embraced your curiosity enough to start seeing patterns. Don't ignore them. See if they inspire you to explore other topics and activities. Go deeper on the ones that are really intriguing to you—follow the bread crumbs and see what else you discover with a topic.

 DETOUR: Sharing your patterns and trends with others

It is early in your journey to think about how you will act like a network or lead like a movement toward shared success at an intersection. For now, we want you to just think about you and where you fit. But, at our firm Potrero Group, we encourage sharing these relationships in the preset #random channel in our Slack workspace, helping our team become exposed to even more ideas. These conversations regularly end up becoming a key part of how we generate results for clients. As we wrote this section, one of our colleagues dropped an Instagram video from daniellabelle1 called "If people did everything in a rush."[9] Watching the hilarity of someone trying to mow their lawn as if they had somewhere to go could be seen by your brain

continued

as just cute and frivolous, and you could quickly move on. As we returned to edit this section over a year later, that resonated even more strongly. Recognizing the pattern of taking time to do things carefully improved our approach to this book. Begin to train your brain to ask, every time, "What does that remind me of from my life, or, perhaps, my 'not-work' list?"

When Daniel ran a residency for theater artists, one of his favorite activities was to spend time shadowing and meeting with artists from different arenas. One time, he even took a group to chat with his dentist about the artistic decisions made in reconstructing a smile. The dentist shared that to make false teeth look natural, he often recommends that his clients not go for perfection but try to match the imperfections unique to their mouth. After all, a reconstructed smile might be advertised as glistening white, but something too pristine is too easily read as fake. The goal is actually not to shine but to appear to be real and natural. In observing someone else's approach to achieve creativity in their work, but with different needs and results, the artists saw a reflection of themselves. They thought about the patterns in their work that led them to try to achieve perfection. But for the audience to relate to their work, it is often the little natural imperfections that make it resonate.

The goal in all of this is to build your pattern recognition skills and then use them to see what is actually going on in your work, not what you think it should be or want it to be. That's why "taking a big step back" is our next skill. More often than not, we need to step back and think about where we could go and see where we are actually going.

CHAPTER 7

Taking a Big Step Back

For most of us, the best way to learn and practice intersection work will be to notice and negotiate with the systems *inside* our organization prior to applying that experience outside it. A good way to do that is to produce a systems map.

Systems mapping is, broadly speaking, drawing the relationships between the people or other things that together make up a system.[1] Their most basic form comes through actor mapping (how key individuals, departments, teams, or organizations are related) and/or issue mapping (how key topics important to a system connect to one another) in a cluster or "brain dump" map, which puts a topic in the middle and sees how actors or issues connect to it and each other. If you focus on your own organization, you can bring your own institutional knowledge to practice seeing how connections are drawn. You can then use your strength in recognizing trends to pretty quickly see them emerge visually, right in front of your eyes.

Practicing taking a big step back

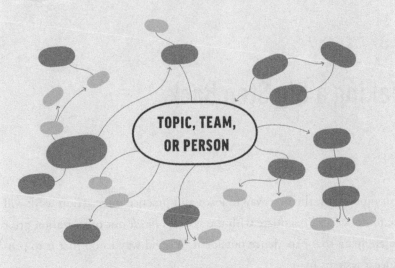

So, to create a systems map for your organization, pick a topic, team, or person that your gut tells you is currently creating dynamism—whether it be excitement or conflict. Grab a large piece of paper or whiteboard and write the topic, team, or person in large letters in the middle and draw a circle around it. Now simply "brain dump" all the people, elements, or ideas that connect to the center of your map. Draw a line to each one. As you add another one that connects to the center, see what else it connects to and draw a line to it too. Who are the partners and the people you would include? What machines and tools are necessary in this system? Before long, don't be worried if you are no longer drawing lines to the center but simply from one new element to another. By the end, it should look quite messy, many lines crossing over each other.

Take a step back and look at it. Are there other elements, beyond the person or topic you put in the center, that have a lot of lines coming out of them? Congratulations! By taking a step back, you may be uncovering something that is quite crucial about the system, perhaps even more so than what you originally put in the center! Draw circles around those things or rewrite them in larger font and circle them.

This is the power of systems mapping. Who and what can be brought to bear that magnify the impact of what you do that you may have not at first noticed? Who and what are connected to those items that might be conduits for you to work with to solve those problems or build those opportunities? Remember, the goal here is to just step back and look. This initial exercise should take you half an hour, or an hour maximum. But perhaps put the map on your office wall, and every so often spend another ten minutes adding words or lines.

A systems map is never truly complete. Think of it like a map of the US highway system—it shows some major routes you can take, but if you zoom in, there is likely to be so many more intricate possibilities of side roads you didn't even notice the first time. We actually think of the zoomed-in area as a network map. The network is all the other routes you may take (just as zooming out may reveal a network you can make between systems!). There are also more complex systems maps you can learn that go deeper in understanding the complexity of the connections you have drawn (look up "causal loops" and "connected circles").

Most systems are set up to provide structure so that the expected result can happen as perfectly and predictably as possible, something that is often found in organizations, particularly as they grow and mature. The goal is to allow those of us within the system to know how to use the system's resources to great advantage. In fact, this is why we learn systems of sorts—driving, business, science, art, you name it—so that we can work within them, and they can be a resource to further success.

Seelos and Mair remind us that in order to accomplish systems-level change work, you must often "climb system peaks."[2] A system peak is a spot you or your organization occupies within a larger system that allows you to begin to see other opportunities for change and impact. Importantly, however, to Seelos and Mair's model, you already need to be an effective contributor in the larger system. You might be only a small contributor—but nonetheless you need to be contributing. Often the small contributions you or your organization makes at one point in time open the way to larger opportunities later. This points to the importance of developing the domain-specific skills that we discussed in chapter 2. It can be extremely challenging to change (or even observe) a system if you don't have competence in at least some parts of the subsystems that compose the larger system. Your work in understanding the systems and subsystems of your organization and its partners will go a long way toward helping you ensure your ability to climb system peaks.

By summiting system peaks, we can recognize what in the current system can and often needs to be subverted (and what needs to be enhanced) to get important work accomplished. A familiar paradox of the workplace is to be called for creativity and innovation but to then be tasked with efficiency and delivery. It seems too often that the system is set up to make the individual irrelevant. As the Industrial Revolution taught us, our bodies are supposed to be cogs in the machine.

This is where being a systems thinker comes in. We've all had that colleague who somehow seems to march to their own drummer, and although you are doing what was tasked, they are the ones rewarded. These are systems thinkers at work within your shared system. Another label for them is "intrapreneurs"—people who push new ideas and create new revenue streams within an organization. While, yes, systems require us to do what is asked of us to keep the stability of the structure, they also are better served when we do what they *need*.

It is why, to continue the car metaphor, you have to get your oil changed according to a schedule. Dirty oil and oil filters reduce your car's performance, including reduced acceleration and engine sputtering. Clean oil keeps engine parts lubricated and keeps gunk out of the engine. But we all know that's just the bare minimum of preventative care. Your car will truly last when you respect every gear and lever within it, taking care of each part as it needs to be cared for. When you think like a system, you extend your reach and impact further than what one person can normally accomplish. Like the car that's well maintained, a system that encourages people to think about what needs to be created by the many partners working at the intersection will produce profits and impact far beyond what was originally envisioned.

This is perhaps a good time to move beyond metaphor into a concrete example of how thinking like a system led to profits and impact in a real-life situation. Our first case study will particularly focus on how the skills we've learned thus far led to this outcome but will also zoom out to remind you of the overall narrative we are following in this book.

CHAPTER 8

Driving Innovation in the Energy Sector

. . . .

The United States uses an astonishing amount of energy. This use will likely continue to soar as consumers use more and larger electronic devices, continue driving long distances for work and leisure, and face the need for more and more climate-controlled homes. The dilemma, of course, is that all this energy consumption is expensive and potentially environmentally damaging. New plants cost millions or billions to build. But current energy production is one of the largest contributors to climate-changing greenhouse gas emissions. With the effects of climate change more and more apparent, pressures to produce clean, cheap energy or reduce energy use will continue to grow.

Despite the increased costs and climate impacts, reducing energy use appears a nearly impossible challenge. Various initiatives in the past have encouraged people to turn down their thermostats in winter and wear a sweater or to live in a warmer home in summer—these initiatives are doomed to fail from the start. People want to live in comfort, and comfort requires significant amounts of energy. Encouraging people to use smaller or fewer devices isn't likely to gain much traction either.

We need to find ways to produce more energy without causing environmental damage or use less energy without giving up comfort. And it needs to be affordable. It is a complex challenge that demands a complex solution.

The answer? Think like a system!

Think like a system

Years ago, a number of states recognized that one of the best ways to generate more energy was to drive innovation in the energy sector. One idea, somewhat radical at the time, was called decoupling. It is a policy solution that recognizes a systems approach to achieving energy conservation—it decouples the relationship between energy consumption and profitability. Traditionally, like most companies, utilities have built-in incentives for consumers to use more energy.[1] Using the skills of thinking like a system, the idea of decoupling is built on the observation that if utilities make more profits when people use more energy, then massive incentives exist for more energy to be used. Decoupling changes these incentives and creates powerful mechanisms for utilities to make fair market profits regardless of whether end users consume or conserve energy.

Decoupling policies have now been adopted by 24 states and the District of Columbia. And the results are powerful. States like California and Vermont that have decoupling policies in place have maintained a nearly constant energy usage per capita for more than 30 years, whereas states without decoupling have steep increases in energy use per capita. One would expect growth in energy usage given the prevalence of new electronic devices, size of televisions, and increased need for air-conditioning. This is exactly what happens in states without decoupling. And why the results in states like California and Vermont are so noteworthy.

Part of the reason why decoupling works so well is that its proponents recognize patterns and trends. For instance, public-sector proponents of decoupling recognize that businesses, universities, and nonprofits all play essential roles in driving innovation. In the past, when regulators tried to force consumers to save energy by turning down thermostats or driving only on some days, the results were certain failure. With decoupling, regulators often work proactively with corporations to make funding available for the development of new technologies, new devices, and new approaches. The result is that less energy is consumed, and consumers are more comfortable and have access to higher-quality energy-efficient products.

A prime example of this approach is the California Lighting Technology Center (CLTC), a self-supporting center of excellence located at UC Davis. The CLTC's goal is to accelerate the development and commercialization of energy-efficient lighting and daylighting technologies. Funded with revenue made available through the decoupling process and membership fees from industry and nonprofit affiliates, the CLTC takes a big step back and analyzes the system at play. They drive innovation by identifying the different contributors on their systems map and connecting those regulators, companies, entrepreneurs, and nonprofit environmental partners.

Act like a network

The CLTC conducts research on state-of-the-art energy-saving technology while simultaneously providing laboratories for research, development, prototyping, and product testing to build pathways between the various players in this system. The CLTC also serves as an intermediary between inventors of new technologies, the regulators who must approve these technologies, and the larger companies that can take the technologies to scale and deploy them in the marketplace. The CLTC employs experts who work between and among the various parts of the system. Particularly effective is the CLTC's work in disseminating the results of the innovation through case studies, white papers, demonstrations, and training and education for professionals in the field. In this way, they are acting like a network, which we will dive into in the next section of our book.

Lead like a movement

Driving systems change is hard partially because the actors in different parts of the system often don't know and trust one another. The CLTC and like organizations can be effective because they recognize system-wide trends and can share them and build trust. For example, regulators are more likely to trust data provided by an organization like the CLTC than from industry. Likewise, the technical experts at the CLTC are often able to present cutting-edge scientific and product information in a way that is appealing to industry but which the government may not have the capability to create. In this way, the CLTC is building a coalition by managing dissonance, incumbents, and secret agendas. These are critical skills to leading like a movement, which we will dive into in our third section of the book.

Reframing for a new way of seeing things

As we move into the second half of our *Think Like a System* skills, you will see ways in which people working at intersections are able to grow their understanding of what they observe and eventually reframe them for a new way of seeing things.

Let's face it, energy is boring. People want energy, lighting, heating, and air-conditioning, and they don't want to think of the details. And yet it is the CLTC's job to think about details and help people (especially regulators, manufacturers, and environmental organizations) see how cutting-edge energy-saving technology can improve society. The

CLTC has created powerful demonstrations of how upgraded hospital lighting can improve patient outcomes, how state-of-the-art lighting can save human lives in cities while saving dramatic amounts of energy, and how new lighting systems can help people feel safer on vast college and corporate campuses. This reframing has proven powerful for getting the new technology adopted. We will dive into this and related skills in the second half of this section.

Conclusion

Thinking like a system isn't easy, but the results can be profound. Utilities that adopt decoupling policies are found to spend more per customer on energy efficiency than utilities that don't decouple,[2] allowing them to simultaneously meet growing energy demands, reduce carbon emissions, and drive innovation for entrepreneurs who are developing and selling amazing new devices and making our homes more comfortable and energy efficient. Working with an organization like the CLTC that bridges different sectors or cultures can be especially helpful in understanding the system and intersection that connects them. They are able to move the whole system forward and create powerful results that would be impossible without a recognition of how everything in the system is connected.

CHAPTER 9

Listening with Empathy and Reflection

. . . .

We're social animals, and we need to harness our social skills to truly interrogate and understand a system. And the specific part of the social we usually think we need to refine is how we speak, but often what we truly need to refine is how we listen.

"There's an important difference between hearing and listening," Leon Berg says in his TED Talk "The Power of Listening—An Ancient Practice for Our Future."[1] Berg is one of the founders of the Ojai Foundation, which is noted for its listening circles, or Councils. "Hearing is one of our natural senses, but listening requires focus and intention." To think like a system and use the powerful leverage a system enables, you need to master empathetic and reflective listening. Too many of us think having a conversation is simply waiting your turn to speak or offer your opinion. This is a crucial mistake. If you are to uncover how the systems around you work, you need to be able to understand what it looks like from perspectives other than your own. You can do this only by clearly offering your full attention and helping others deliver their information to you as clearly and fully as possible.

Every one of us has been in a place where someone may be hearing us, but they are clearly not listening. The sound is clearly reaching their ears and they may even be nodding, but their eyes and attention are directed elsewhere in the room or perhaps within their own head. Art Markman, at the University of Texas at Austin, points out that the structure of a basic conversation supports hearing but not listening. One person speaks, while the other is silent. Then the second person contributes their thoughts on the topic. The fatal flaw is that we train our brains to spend time planning what we want to say next instead of listening to what is being said to us. The sneaky success of listening is not that it changes your opinion but that you are able to form an opinion from a full perspective—yours and the speaker's. You can think, "They said *this* . . . but I actually think *that*." If you hadn't listened, you might not have ever assessed how you feel and why you feel it.

Many would say the sign of a good listener is someone who is open to being convinced by what another says. Unfortunately, we as a species aren't that good at change, so we aren't usually open to being convinced by what someone says (check out your social media feed if you don't believe us). *Empathetic* listening is actually quite a simple concept—it is acknowledging and validating whatever feelings someone else has. You don't need to be convinced. You can use body language to nod, smile, frown, lean in, or simply make eye contact, or use a nonverbal vocalization like a "hm," "mm," or "oh." *Reflective* listening is just one step further. Your role, as a listener, is to tell the other person what you think they are saying and then, ideally, to help them better understand or convey their thoughts.

A study by Israeli organizational behavior scholars Guy Itzchakov and Avraham N. Kluger found that the result of good listening is found not with the listener but in what happens to the speaker, who feels less anxious and gains higher clarity about their opinions on topics and a stronger desire to share their feelings on the issue.[2] This sounds like a gift you are giving another person, and it certainly is, but it is also a gift to yourself. By enabling another person's true and clear understanding of something, you bring yourself into a better understanding of your own opinion. In intersection work, we have to look around and try to recognize the choices others are encountering, as well. That will in turn allow us to see our own place and the best choice more fully.

Itzchakov and Kluger list a few, perhaps quite familiar, skills to practice to hone your listening. The first three we list here are really empathetic listening skills: simply acknowledging and validating, using your body language or nonverbal vocalizations.

■➤ GIVE 100 PERCENT OF YOUR ATTENTION.

■➤ DON'T JUDGE.

■➤ DON'T JUMP TO OFFERING A SOLUTION.

The last is where you begin to be reflective.

■➤ ASK MORE QUESTIONS.

To do that, we recommend you turn to Six Sigma.

 Practicing listening with empathy and reflection

Six Sigma training features the concept of the "5 Whys" to determine the operational root cause of an error or problem.[3] To avoid fixing just a symptom and not the root problem, you need to dig deeper and develop a solution that will have a broad impact. To do this effectively, like a curious, if somewhat annoying, child, you first have to keep asking why.

When we're solving a problem, it's one thing to allow someone to feel heard, but that doesn't necessarily reveal a solution. To do that, you need to actively enable that person to look for the root cause. You need to ask them why. When they respond, summarize or rephrase for them what you think you heard them say. Ask if you are correct. Then ask why again. Why

continued

they believe what they believe. Why they feel the way they do. Repeat the process until you reach the root problem. It may take only two or three whys, but most often you'll ask why five or so times. And in the process, you'll learn so much about what you think.

Of course, part of reflective listening is to be attuned to what a person may or may not need in that moment. We will be discussing feedback in chapter 25, so here we'll just say that sometimes a person simply wants to vent, and that's OK. Don't be afraid to ask them what they want. Would it be helpful for them if you helped them find the cause, or would they rather have good, old-fashioned empathy? Sometimes "that must be really hard for you" and a pat on the back is all they need.

Daniel has coined what he calls "SEER" communication skills, which introduce verbal elements of speed and enunciation and pair them with listening elements of empathy and reflection. One of the reminders he has found useful when working with organizations or business students is to remind them to also not be afraid to fake it at first. You may need to force a response, even if it is not actually how you feel. Treat it as a technical skill first. If you are uncomfortable making eye contact, for instance, practice staring at a spot between their eyes. It will get you used to the action, even if it may feel fake at first, for them and for you. The same goes for the "5 Whys." Perhaps your mind wandered, and you weren't truly listening. A well-placed "why" can get you back on track!

This is why a useful tool for empathetic and reflective listening shows up in an operational root cause analysis. Like operations, intersections are complicated systems, with each partner having their own interests and needs. If you learn to listen to collaborators empathetically and reflectively, you will help unite across different silos. JMW Consultants focuses on organizational, team, and project performance. Associate consultant Elyse Maltin notes in *Harvard Business Review* that when working with public-private partnerships, the company rarely saw parties reveal independent interests that went beyond mutually agreed-upon shared goals.[4] This leads to a rush to judgment on the unexpected behavior of one party from another, escalating rapidly the inevitable conflict that comes from such multifaceted work. We are left to wonder if they simply didn't push each other to get to the root cause. To rephrase what they heard and to ask why. Genuinely wanting to know how another person thinks truly helps you find out what you think. That lays the groundwork for everything to come and leverages the enormous benefits of working as part of a broader system to get your work accomplished.

Listening, of course, is not the only way we understand and interpret the signals others are putting out. There are even more subtle ways we can connect with one another. And recognizing those can be the most challenging, and most rewarding, ways of understanding the systems we encounter.

CHAPTER 10

Tapping into Intuition

Thus far, we've discussed using sight and hearing in *Think Like a System*, but now we want to turn to one of the least understood of our senses— our intuition, or our sixth sense. Intuition involves processing knowledge we gain through observation without being aware that we are processing it. Those vague feelings or hunches most of us experience help us access what we know but can't easily explain. This knowledge is essential to seeing the world around you as a system.

We colloquially call this "going with your gut." In sports there is a big debate between older coaches who go with their guts and younger coaches who use data to drive their decisions. This is happening, albeit less in the public eye, in the boardroom too. As a result, many of us discount these intuitive moments, but stories shared by leaders are often filled with reports of listening to their gut in order to make big decisions or avoid giant catastrophes. But we'd argue there may be less of a divide than the generations may think. A well-developed intuition may come from simply having experience and subconsciously recognizing a pattern.

Harvard Business School professor Laura Huang, over a series of studies, observed hundreds of venture capitalists who went with gut feel even when the market data or other financial information told them otherwise. Many failed, but also many were successful. An intuition can serve you as a sense; like when you use your other senses, it is based on information you are receiving. Huang learned that successful "go with your gutters" understood that it is not just about going with an impulse but cultivated with experience. They commit to practicing this sense, just like practicing listening, by paying attention to patterns and prototypes in their field and linking them to future decisions.[1] We'd perhaps call this another thing—thinking like a system!

The process of how intuition plays out in our professional life can be visualized by using the metaphor of an iceberg, originally conceived by anthropologist Edward T. Hall. The idea is that above the symbolic water-line are the things we can see and observe about a culture. Within your

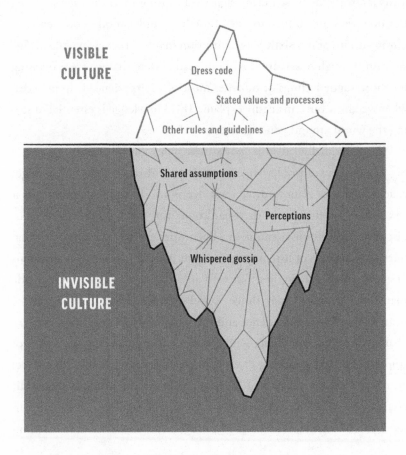

organization, that might be the company's stated values and processes, the dress code, and other rules and guidelines HR is in charge of ensuring everyone knows. Underneath the waterline lies the rest of the iceberg: a giant mass of unspoken shared assumptions, perceptions, and whispered gossip, just waiting to break our ship in half. Your company may say it values innovation but overly punishes people who make mistakes. It says it values work-life balance, but those who choose to work from home see far fewer promotions. This invisible culture is actually typically much larger and more significant than what is visible. If you are on the *Titanic*, things aren't going to go well for you if you don't recognize what's invisible.

If our intuition tells us something is lurking underneath the water, but we don't have any logic to back it up, our instinct often is to ignore it. We can generally apply logic only to what our five senses tell us. But our intuition, based on experience and practice, tells us otherwise. Recognizing patterns, empathetically and reflectively listening, and taking a step back will all fall flat if we don't follow our intuition and instead just look at what we can see above the surface. A great visual to think of is a forest—there is a lot of complexity of that system aboveground to look at. By the time you are done mapping the relationship between the predators and prey and the plants as their habitats, you would think you'd know the system pretty well. But have you ever seen an image of tree roots under the ground? It's a systems map unto itself. You can't see it—but you have to rely on your intuition it is there in order to truly think like a system.

 ## Practicing tapping into intuition

When working at an intersection, you are no longer in your own forest or your own cruise ship. All you might be able to see is what's above. You will need to link your decisions to patterns and prototypes you've researched

continued

from systems you are familiar with or are comfortable in, where you have a better ability to unearth what's below. So, to refine your intuition for intersection work, start by applying it to better understanding your own organization or team. On a sheet of paper, draw an iceberg, noting the waterline (be sure to put most of the iceberg below the water). Around the tip of the iceberg, write your organization's or team's written processes for collaboration. Feel free to copy from any documentation you have on the processes (it's not a test, after all). What has to be included in contracts, other agreements, or meeting minutes, for example? Next you'll write what you intuitively know about these processes below the waterline on your paper. What have you heard people say when you've actively listened? What have you seen when you were curiously observing? Most importantly, what are you sensing is not being said or shown but you know to be true? What are those things you can't back up with facts, can't quite explain how you know? Write those down.

Study what's below. What are some things you think are pretty common to other organizations in your field or teams in your company? How about fields or companies outside your own? What is unique to your team, organization, or field? When you start working with collaborators at an intersection of sectors, you might draw an iceberg for them. Or better yet, if you feel comfortable, ask them to draw it for themselves. You will be developing your intuition the only way you can grow anything—practice.

As you get more practiced at intersection work, you will want to skip this step, but that assumption that your intuition is fully aware of what lies below can be dangerous. This is when the younger data-driven generation gets frustrated—you still need to study the data! You need to do whatever you can to reduce the odds of disaster. Because intersections don't have just one cruise ship in the water—they have many. The level of complexity of multiple partners from multiple systems makes for more complexity, and more people and institutions hurt if things go wrong.

It is only after you have fully oriented yourself to your new intersection environment and recognized your internal reactions that you'll be able to use your systems thinking skills to tell a story of what you see in a way that can begin to draw in others. This leads us to our final skill of this section, which will lay the groundwork to begin to act like a network and gather momentum with your collaborators at an intersection.

CHAPTER 11

Reframing for a New Way of Seeing Things

. . . .

"Framing" means to construct meaning for an action or series of actions that relates to the ideas, values, and belief systems of the people working in an initiative. That's a fancy way of saying that framing sets the agenda for the work of the initiative. By using words, phrases, visions, and worldviews, the person framing the conversation can move the work in a powerful new direction. Leaders do this all the time and, unsurprisingly, those speeches or texts tend to stand out in our history textbooks. "Ask not what your country can do for you, but what you can do for your country." "I have a dream." "We hold these truths to be self-evident." It's also critical to getting important work accomplished and moving people through the inevitable hardships that are a part of transformative work. Each of these quotes acknowledges challenges—a country not doing enough, a reality that's not good enough, a truth that does not need to be proven. They look at the same world as the people who feel this hopelessness and they offer an alternative way of looking at things. In intersection environments, you're often moving against the well-worn paths of people who are used to working in their own self-reinforcing silos, unable to see how the world could be any different. You have an opportunity to show them otherwise.

In fact, what John F. Kennedy, Martin Luther King Jr., and Thomas Jefferson did with these turns of phrase is not just framing but *re*framing.

When Daniel was directing plays, he used to start each production with a collection of visual art, music, historical photographs, and major themes and ideas that he felt were at the core of the text. Of course, the written play itself provided its own frame. Each individual reads it and reacts to it. But when putting on a production of it, you need to *re*frame it so that the actors and those working behind the scenes can be on the same page.

Before discussing what he wanted to *do* with the text, he endeavored to showcase what he felt the text was trying to *say*. Partly this was to get everyone on the same page. But more importantly, it was a way for him to make sense of the system of the play. He would even try to get the ideas of the play down to one sentence. Daniel could then ask the designers on his team to do their own research based on this inspiration, which would bring a new shape to the play that built on a solid, clear foundation. He also gave his actors a useful reframe within which to act, motivating their actions and keeping them focused. When done right, this allowed a play that had been produced many times across the country to still motivate a group of artists to perform it. It was still the same play, but its reframing motivated everyone's ability to give it new life.

The ultimate goal of reframing, then, becomes not just to present a vision but to also engender a conversation from your collaborators that could create an even stronger reframe. Often conversations between intersection partners become stuck in participants' prior limitations and constraints rather than exploring new opportunities and freedoms. The job of reframing is to see possibilities in a new light. As a leader working at the intersection, you will need to always be thinking about how you can reframe conversations to advance what may be an uncomfortable process for many participants. When you set the reframe up to acknowledge the complexity of the system at work, ideas and ways of doing work will collide and overlap.

One tool for learning this skill comes, not surprisingly, from outside your silo. Will Mancini offers a unique perspective of intersection work as a pastor turned consultant and coach in his book *Church Unique: How Missional Leaders Cast Vision, Capture Culture, and Create Movement* (2008). Jumping off the idea that "words create worlds," Mancini reframes the idea of a church's mission quite literally in his Vision Frame. The Vision Frame has four sides: the Missional Mandate (what you are *ultimately* supposed to be doing in your work), the Missional Motive (the shared convictions that guide your actions), the Missional Map (a process of how you will accomplish your mandate to the fullest impact possible), and Missional Life Marks (a set of attributes in an individual's life that reflect accomplishment in the mandate). Inside of this frame, you'll find your Missional Mountaintop. He points out that the four sides could easily just be called Mission, Values, Strategy, and Measures, showcasing the business approach underlying his customer-centric language. But in this case, the customer is an individual seeking a closer relationship to God, so Mancini pushes churches to work within this higher calling that he knows they, and the customers with jobs to be done, can better relate to. By doing so, he is reframing the idea of a church's missionary work and showing his readers how to reframe their own ideas of missionary work to inspire business success.

Of course, you don't have to search for ideas about how other silos approach their work at intersections; intersections naturally provide reframing opportunities. The magic of negotiating one business or sector's context with another's is that a new light shines both on the meaning of your own work and the original work it was associated with. Think about how SpaceX has collaborated with NASA to redefine space travel as something that could be associated with tourism and personal adventure. Framing allowed a nation to believe they can put a human on the moon. Reframing allowed private citizens like you and me to believe we might actually be that human. It may not be what John F. Kennedy envisioned in his wildest dreams when he first proposed putting a man on the moon, but it lends even more power to the idea. Kennedy's powerful frame has lasted the test of time because it took into account the systematic relationship between government and taxpayers working together for a shared goal. SpaceX was simply able to reframe the idea from a business perspective.

Practicing reframing for a new way of seeing things

The best way to practice reframing is to think of a favorite hobby, one you know quite deeply. Let's say you are a huge tennis fan. How does your vision for solving your intersection problem map onto tennis? Perhaps there is a sense that each time you try to solve the problem, it feels like the problem returns the ball just a little farther out of your reach. Or perhaps the problem feels like being a tennis fan, snapping your head back and forth over and over, seeing two disagreeing opponents dueling back and forth until both are exhausted. Thinking about your problem differently can at least present the problem more clearly, if not inspire a solution. The core point here is that your frame of reference defines your worldview. If you allow yourself and your partners to see your work within one frame of reference, you're imposing undue limitations on your potential for creative action. By reframing the situation, you are creating many new possibilities for you and your partners.

Systems are everywhere you look, as are the opportunities to overlap them or create new ones. Just one random example—the next time you watch a TV or movie streaming service, think about how it is organized as a system you use in your leisure time, with its self-starting videos and endless recommendations to keep you watching. How do those observations connect to other systems in your life? Find someone with whom to talk about it!

Setting yourself up to recognize patterns and trends on your own and sharing your reframe with others is just the beginning of growing your intersection tool kit. It is the bridge to acting like a network and leading like a movement.

With that, let's wrap this section with another case study, one that will review the recent *Think Like a System* skills we learned and prepare us to start our next section, *Act Like a Network*.

CHAPTER 12

Starting a Revolution in Healthy Food

· ·

What do you do when you're unhappy with the status quo? You start a revolution, of course. In the case of Kristin Groos and Kirsten Tobey, two business school friends, their revolution was to transform school lunches with nutritious food that kids would enjoy. Their vehicle for the revolution was a for-profit food service start-up called Revolution Foods, initially focused on serving healthy school lunches.

The challenge was that neither of Revolution Foods's founders had significant food service experience nor significant financial assets. They overcame those challenges by thinking like a system, acting like a network, and leading like a movement. The results have been extraordinary. Starting Revolution Foods in 2006 with serving food to kids in a few charter schools in Oakland, California, Groos and Tobey built a company that, as of 2022, serves over two million healthy meals to families and children in schools and communities throughout the United States. According to their website, they have distributed nearly a half billion meals across 23 states, have an annual revenue of over $130 million, and employ over 1,500 people across the nation. Revolution Foods also serves senior programs, community feeding programs, and many other venues and, additionally, offers a line of healthy packaged food items available in 4,000 grocery stores nationwide. In 2021, they were named one of the ten most innovative companies by *Fast Company*, joining the top-100 list for the third time in a decade.

While Groos and Tobey utilized many of the skills this book covers, this case study focuses on the three transferable skills we just covered that they used to think like a system: *Listening with Empathy and Reflection*, *Tapping into Intuition*, and *Reframing for a New Way of Seeing Things*.

Listening with empathy and reflection

Breaking into any new market is a formidable task. This is exponentially more formidable in the marketplace of serving food in schools. Traditionally, school lunches were procured, prepared, and served on-site by school cafeteria workers employed by the school district. Outside food vendors were not typically welcome to bid for school lunch contracts. Over time, to save money and resources, more and more schools started outsourcing food service to large conglomerates that run massive centralized food preparation and distribution systems. It is hard to enter the soft drink market when there is already Coke and Pepsi operating at scale for a fraction of your cost and an advertising budget as big as some countries' GDP. This is akin to the world that Groos and Tobey had to enter in our school cafeterias. What's more, further adding to the challenges of entering the school lunch market, school food systems are highly regulated by the government with low price points. In other words, you can't undersell the big budget competition even if by some miracle you did find a way to beat them at their own game.

Thinking about the system (taking a big step back), one might quickly notice that the result of this highly centralized approach to food service is that much of the food served in the nation's schools is low quality, unappealing, and lacking nutrition. There was a need there, and the leaders of Revolution Foods listened to it. Rather than conducting national focus groups, they started by talking directly to the parents of children enrolled in local charter schools. They heard stories of frustration over the quality of the food, unresponsive bureaucracies, and kids going hungry because they didn't want to eat the food served to them. Revolution Foods leadership, rather than corporate focus group consultants, conducted the meetings, and they responded with empathy and understanding. Based on the meetings, they were able to work with their local Whole Foods store to develop sample meals. Then they met with kids to test the meals, challenging their initial assumptions gathered from the parents. Based on the listening and feedback, they were able to quickly iterate and change the meal approach in real time. The kids noticed the changes, and many felt, for the first time, that their tastes and concerns were taken seriously.

These extensive listening sessions with charter school parents and kids were essential to the growth of Revolution Foods. By listening with empathy and reflection, Groos and Tobey learned valuable lessons about the food service system. Once the kids and parents realized that Revolution Foods was serious about observing and learning to make healthy food that kids liked, the buzz about them increased. The positive feedback they received helped them gain an early foothold into the highly engaged system of the charter school network. This system comprised many of the most vocal and active parents in a community. More and more parents began lobbying school systems for Revolution Foods to be offered in their schools, and their business started growing. Having these parents praise Revolution Foods to their communities ultimately helped pave the way to entry into many other non-charter school systems, a tight market that many competitors couldn't secure. Ultimately, Revolution Foods was able to land contracts in many large traditional school districts like Denver, Washington, DC, and San Francisco.

Tapping into intuition

One of the important early decisions Groos and Tobey needed to make was around the legal structure for Revolution Foods. Should the company be formed as a mission-driven nonprofit organization, or should they organize as a for-profit venture? It was an agonizing decision—a nonprofit structure would allow Revolution Foods to access philanthropic grants and would give them early access to financial capital. Groos and Tobey had worked in nonprofits and were familiar with the culture of them and the trust that they engendered with many community groups and governmental institutions. Conversely, the pair recognized that a for-profit legal structure would likely allow the company to scale more easily and reach more students faster. Further, the for-profit structure might allow them to attract, hire, and retain stronger talent because of higher pay and profit-sharing options.

After a lot of soul-searching and research about the appropriate structures, the pair decided to trust their intuition that a nonprofit structure would limit their growth opportunities. Of course, all good intuitions are informed by what you can see so you can guess at what you can't see. In making the final decision, Groos and Tobey sought the counsel of one of their business school professors, Will Rosenzweig, who had played founding or senior roles in many leading healthy food brands like The Republic of Tea and Odwalla. Rosenzweig was well familiar with the trade-offs between nonprofit and for-profit legal approaches and gave them important insights and advice. Thus, Groos and Tobey were able to build on what Rosenzweig had seen in the past to aid in their decision-making. Ultimately, the pair decided on a for-profit structure. They haven't looked back.

Reframing for a new way of seeing things

The journey to make any start-up successful is full of twists and turns. Revolution Foods had already reframed the school lunch market away from cost efficiency and toward healthy-eating movements found on supermarket shelves. Yet rarely does a company experience a shock as great as a global pandemic to truly have to completely shift how they see their business. Heavily reliant on schools for the majority of its funding, Revolution Foods faced an existential crisis in 2020 when schools suddenly closed and almost all learning went online. The bottom fell out of their operating model.

Not surprisingly, the leadership team of Revolution Foods went into emergency-planning mode to save the business and continue providing healthy food. Ultimately, they reframed their business as "transforming citywide wellness by making healthy food accessible for all."[1] This reframing allowed Revolution Foods to quickly pivot their business model to serve seniors, homeless communities, and others hard-hit by the pandemic. The reframing made perfect sense because Revolution Foods had large culinary centers, a strong distribution network, and deep experience in providing healthy food in diverse settings. Revolution Foods also had competencies in government payment and reimbursement systems, allowing them to utilize the significant financial resources the government was deploying to serve society's most vulnerable communities during the pandemic.

This reframing by Revolution Foods allowed them to better utilize the systems of which they're a part and which they've built to strengthen their business and serve millions of meals to those most in need. Had they not utilized such skillful reframing, the result may have been very different for the company, and many at-risk people would not have received their healthy, high-quality food at such a critical time in the world.

Conclusion

Many entrepreneurs get ahead of themselves and become obsessed by their idea. They seek funding and strong financial returns before they understand the system in which they operate—and hence waste valuable time, money, and effort. Groos and Tobey stand in sharp contrast. Because Groos and Tobey didn't have large war chests of initial funding, they needed to think like a system to survive. The results are stunning. Two business students indeed started a revolution. What began as a disruptive idea is now employing thousands, generating millions in revenue, and transforming health across the country.

We've reviewed how leaders think like a system to position themselves for success at an intersection. Next let's learn what they do. This is what we call *Act Like a Network*.

PART 2

ACT LIKE A NETWORK

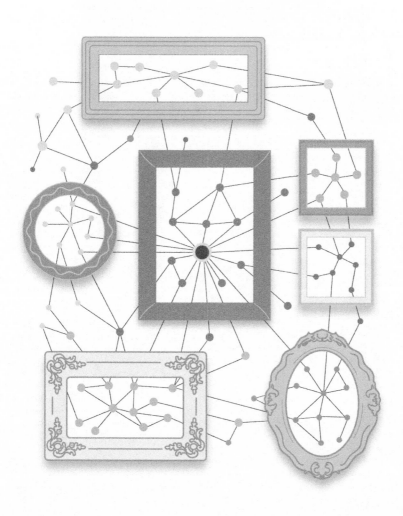

CHAPTER 13

Act Like a Network Overview

· ·

Act Like a Network is the name we give to the second group of skills necessary to prepare for your work at an intersection. We often drive work forward in ways that are comfortable to us, and usually, we need to be alone to feel that way. Yet this approach denies us the profound opportunities of working with others and the rewards of bringing others' perspectives, experience, and networks to bear on the work. By doing the work ourselves, we may feel more control, but we don't see our own limitations, and we miss out on ideas and worldviews that produce an impact greater than the sum of its parts.

The skills we will discuss in this section build the connective tissue between silos that can fill your intersection with all the talent you need to be successful.

Here's an important note: people often confuse acting like a network with networking. Networking is a business activity of connecting with other people you have something in common with or who are interesting to you for the purpose of promoting yourself, your company, or your wares. Acting like a network means intentionally designing and building a network for the purpose of taking your work to the next level. It will include a deep assessment of your skills, talents, and assets so that you can identify people and organizations that would make good partners for the intersection work you want to do. It's not a small lift, granted, but it's well worth doing.

Before exploring the skills of acting like a network, we suggest you get your initial ideas in writing. A one-page summary is fine—answer with short phrases. You can use a simple format:

- ➤ WHAT ARE YOU TRYING TO ACCOMPLISH WITH YOUR INTERSECTION WORK?

- ➤ WHY SHOULD ANYONE CARE ABOUT WHAT YOU'RE TRYING TO ACCOMPLISH?

- ➤ WHO IS OR WILL BE YOUR TEAM AND PARTNERS, AND WHY HAVE YOU INCLUDED THEM?

- ➤ WHEN WILL YOU BE READY TO DELIVER?

- ➤ WHAT ARE YOUR MILESTONES?

- ➤ WHO ELSE DO YOU NEED? THINK BROADLY IN TERMS OF SKILL SETS.

- ➤ WHAT BLIND SPOTS DO YOU HAVE? IDENTIFY YOUR HUNCH ABOUT YOUR BLIND SPOTS AND ASK FOR HELP IDENTIFY-ING OTHERS.

Once you've completed this personal brainstorming, use it as a chance to meet and discuss with people in your current network. Don't think about your potential or current intersection partners just yet—think about people you trust, who know you, and/or who know the sectors in which you want to work (though you may find those people might naturally become one and the same). You can send them your initial ideas to read in advance or just summarize it with them. When you meet, ask as many follow-up questions of them as you can, such as the following:

- ➤ WHAT DO YOU THINK ABOUT THE IDEAS?

- ➤ WHAT DID I MISS?

➡ **WHAT DO *YOU* THINK MY BLIND SPOTS ARE?**

➡ **WHO ELSE SHOULD I MEET TO GET MORE FEEDBACK?**

➡ **WHO AT THE INTERSECTION NEEDS TO BE INVOLVED TO REACH THESE MILESTONES?**

This isn't a time to debate the feedback you receive. Just listen and learn. This is the first and most essential part of building the network. Ideally conduct at least 20 of these meetings if you're seriously considering a new initiative. From there, you can plot out the areas of agreement and disagreement in what you've heard. Where there's disagreement, ask more questions. (This is a great time to break out your "5 Whys"!) Once you understand the root cause of the disagreement, you will likely have uprooted the blind spots—the what you didn't know you didn't know.

Once you feel you've uprooted your blind spots and, perhaps, been able to reframe your challenge (maybe in a single sentence), you are now ready to purposely design a network that can help you accomplish your goal. Building on the systems map you drew in chapter 7, you'll want to draw a network map now. View your systems map as your solar system—you are the sun, and there are planets that orbit around you. A network map makes you realize that there are thousands of other solar systems in our galaxy (as of this writing, there are around 3,200).[1] So a network map is just a systems map zoomed out. How are you and the people in your system (whether that be a team, a department, or your whole organization) connected to other people who might support the intersection work you want to accomplish? Literally drawing dots between you and the others you'll need can help you visualize the network you must create. Who are the people needed? How can you get to them? If you require a lot of tools, technology, and other nonhuman additions to your network, draw these into the network too.

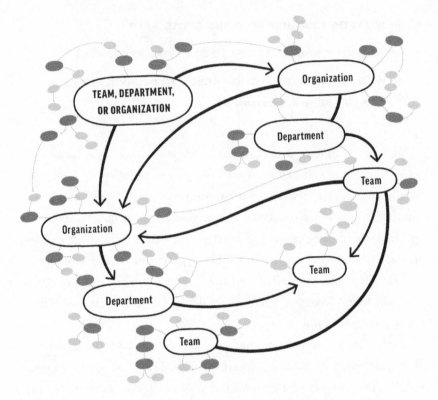

Most great initiatives started with what was, in essence, a network map, even if it never left the person's head who initiated the network. And while they almost always change along the way, the more you can get on paper, the better. It will help you with your blind spots and help you avoid networking with people with similar skills. Instead, you will build a network of people with networks of their own and skills to get you where you want to go. Being deliberate and conscious about your work will help immensely. Before you realize it, your own personal solar system will suddenly feel like a galaxy. To infinity, and beyond. We're not in Kansas anymore. You get it.

DETOUR: Expanding how you see your network

Here are two more, very different takes on envisioning your network that might be fun to try.

Practice expanding your imagination. Imagine ways that you can zero in on the nature of your work not through your work but by imagining a whole network at play to make the work stronger. Think of yourself as the hero in the children's book *Harold and the Purple Crayon*. "One evening, after thinking it over for some time, Harold decided to go for a walk in the moonlight," Crockett Johnson starts his book about a four-year-old, imaginative child.[2] Harold's problem is there isn't a moon or a path to walk on, so he starts by drawing what he needs. Before long, Harold realizes he is not getting anywhere on this straight path. He begins to draw the obstacles and stakeholders of his world. He draws a dragon to guard apples he wants so that they have time to ripen before he is tempted to pick them, and he draws a moose and porcupine to share his leftover food with when he realizes he has too much.

Start with a blank page and draw the world you want with your purple crayon. Who are the partners, people, machines, and tools you would draw if you veered off the straight path and looked at the whole map?

Another tool you can use to create that map is based on the work of Professor Andrew Hargadon (see our authors' note). Dr. Hargadon's term "netstorming" focuses on a network's ability to make the difference between a creative solution being adopted by the public or being completely forgotten.

The steps to netstorming are straightforward:

1. Identify your solution.

2. For 15 minutes, brainstorm as many network partners you already have or need (customers, suppliers, etc.) as possible.

continued

3. For 15 minutes, identify specific people or companies for potential network partners that have not yet been connected to the work. Are they connected to any existing partners?

4. For 15 minutes, brainstorm the connection between your needs and their resources and vice versa.

5. Ask yourself, how can your solution enable those connections?

In our consulting work, we undertake netstorming regularly. For example, our company's mission is to transform organizations working at the intersection of business, government, and nonprofit sectors. We need to continually stay abreast of initiatives where we can add value in those areas where we primarily want to have impact. In one recent netstorming exercise, we were looking to expand our impact on large-scale conservation and environmental change initiatives. A couple of our team members first spent about 15 minutes quickly brainstorming on a whiteboard the companies, environmental organizations, and government agencies working on large-scale conservation initiatives where we knew people or had connections. We then spent about 15 minutes brainstorming those organizations and companies that we wanted to connect with in order to have the impact we wanted. Then we spent another 15 minutes brainstorming (with the help of LinkedIn) connections between the people we had a connection with and those we wanted in the new network we were creating for impact. We spent about five more minutes brainstorming how we might add value to the new connections, were they to become more a part of our existing network.

Finally, in the last step, we spent 15 more minutes brainstorming specific strategies for engaging the highest-priority partners we identified. Sometimes this involves reaching out through our existing network and asking for an introduction. Sometimes it involves sending introductions ourselves. Sometimes we try to meet the people at a conference or public event.

We undertake this process several times a year, especially at the beginning of a new initiative or project. We encourage you to do the same. You'll be amazed at the outcome. You'll meet great new colleagues, spend your time more efficiently, and begin seeing new results in your work.

Of course, building a network brings a whole new set of voices, which in turn brings in a whole new set of challenges. That's why we don't advocate just thinking like a network but also acting like one—that is, working in coordination with others. This is a group of skills that definitely takes hands-on, interactive practice. We'll explore the necessary skills throughout the rest of this part of the book. In the following six chapters, we'll take a deeper dive into each of the skills, devoting a chapter to each skill:

- Acting as a part of a whole
- Getting out of your silo
- Learning other professional languages
- Code-mixing with intention
- Understanding hidden power
- Rewarding risk

We promise your risk will be rewarded if you turn the page!

CHAPTER 14

Acting as a Part of a Whole

. . . .

One of the advantages of acting like a network is that not only does it bring in new people, but it also brings in new tools and skills. Organizational consulting firm SYPartners calls this our "collective creativity." As CEO Jessica Orkin said in 2020, "This time is revealing our essential interdependence. . . . The myth of the solo hero shatters. . . . We are no longer in that world. We are in this one. The wicked problems and complexity of this time demand a more collective approach to leadership and creating new ways forward."[1]

The point is, in our work, we always must be thinking of who or what elements we can add to the network to enhance the collaboration of our team and efficacy of our outcome. Let's return to driving instructor Harold Smith. For Smith, safe and effective driving, once you've allowed the space and visibility of what we call *Think Like a System*, is enhanced by noticing and making eye contact with the other drivers on the road, such as those on the side of the road who may try to merge into your lane or open their door into traffic. A "friendly tap of the horn" is Smith's way of building a collective approach to an effective driving network.[2]

More directly to our topic, Stephen Goldsmith and William D. Eggers, in their book titled *Governing by Network: The New Shape of the Public Sector* (2004), offer ways to act as a part of a whole by asking questions like these:

➡ **WHO ELSE CAN DO THIS BETTER OR DIFFERENTLY?**

➡ **WHAT CAN I LEARN FROM OTHERS?**

➡ **WHAT ARE THE ESSENTIAL PARTS OF THIS WORK FOR ME OR MY ORGANIZATION TO BE IN CHARGE OF?**

➡ **CAN I BRING IN NEW, CREATIVE, OR DIFFERENT PARTNERS FROM WHOM WE'LL LEARN NEW APPROACHES AND GAIN INSIGHTS INTO NEW NETWORKS?**

Yet we are a society obsessed with solo acts (Americans in particular). We love when a singer leaves a band and breaks out on their own. We applaud athletes who "carry their team on their backs." In business, we respond to so-called mavericks like Elon Musk or Jeff Bezos who seemingly get things done by their sheer audacity and force of will.

This brings to mind psychologist Robert Zajonc's mere-exposure effect. Participants in a Zajonc study were shown a variety of plain images and nonsense words, things that would draw very little reaction. As it turned out, the mere exposure to something multiple times was found to be directly correlated with the pleasure felt by the participant, no matter how useless or benign that something was.[3] In other words, things that are familiar make us happy, even when they are not the best option. This may explain the reason most of us are not likely to seek exposure to new things or ideas on our own, instead enjoying the "way it's always been done" even if it's not to our benefit. To set ourselves up for success, we need to build our comfort with the new. Our ability to find entrepreneurial and innovative solutions as "solo acts" perhaps relies strongly on a wide variety of perspectives coming into contact with one another and sharing their independently narrow worldviews that, when combined, may prove useful for our wide collective problems. The hidden geniuses beyond these shining stars could be the manager who brought the band together, the front office executive or coach who built the team, or the investor or chief operating officer who found the right mix of talent to let the CEO shine.

In *Cracking the Network Code*, from chapter 3, there is a beautiful nugget that showcases the power of acting as a part of a whole, delivered by David Haskell, the former regional director for Habitat for Humanity International in the Middle East and East Africa. He points out how people in under-resourced parts of the world can serve as models for building networks.

> You have to make ends meet, so you are always finding solutions in suboptimal conditions. But beauty comes out of this. Imagine that you were tiling a floor. You could use uniform tiles that all fit together nicely but are rather expensive. Or, if you cannot afford those tiles, you can make a mosaic of discarded tile shards. It winds up far more beautiful and functional than the fine tiles. That's the picture of how you do this networked approach. . . . You look around, take stock of the broken and missing pieces, figure out how you can support each other, develop trusting relationships so everyone will work together and hang in there, and you finally create a multiparty collaborative effort that produces better results than a simple grantor-grantee relationship will ever achieve.[4]

 Practicing acting as a part of a whole

A simple network brainstorm can be illustrative. On a piece of paper or in an Excel spreadsheet, list the names of 20–30 people you admire and find interesting. Next to their names, list their occupation, company, and location. Next, try to identify how they might be able to help with your work and one another's. Follow this up by introducing two people who can help each other. That help may or may not indirectly serve you. Rather than practicing the traditional networking ask that puts our needs in the spotlight, we are acting as a part of the whole, helping two others help each other. Your little boat in the water may get farther as a result.

Acting as a part of the whole is not about sacrificing your needs for others. Nor is it charity work. It's an elevation of your work and your impact. It's how you get things done. It isn't, however, about simply surrounding yourself with people who have different ideas. You need to start adopting their best practices and their learnings, and incorporating their networks into your own. The next few skills provide you the tools to do just that.

CHAPTER 15

Getting Out of Your Silo

. . . .

As a professional, you likely work with people who share your occupation, and therefore you will co-create a work culture based on your shared profession. If you are an engineer, you are probably surrounded by other engineers all day. If you are in marketing, most of your meetings are likely filled with other people trained to think about how to make consumers more aware of your product or service. You can go to engineering conferences and marketing conferences and network to the point of exhaustion, but it won't allow you to act like a network. To learn to act like a network, you need to learn about others' perspectives and broaden your own. Marketing people need to see the world through the ordered logic of an engineer. Engineers need to see the products they build beyond efficiency and quality to consider market appeal. Doing this allows you to see your work with fresh eyes. There can be immense learning in this space, which can sometimes be uncomfortable or even triggering. But if you work through that discomfort, you'll truly gain a new perspective.

To explain the effect of professional or sector silos, it's probably about time we look at actual silos. Take your pick—there are the ones that store grain, woodchips, and so forth on farms, and there are, famously, ones that store missiles. Professional silos are more like the latter. All missiles have a single purpose—to hurt an enemy. Likewise, most divisions of an organization have a single purpose—to help the company make money.

But no leader in their right mind would want to launch a single missile without knowing if the other missiles are ready to go too. But if you work in one silo, you are told to just focus on that one missile. This is a profound disconnect—if our leaders need to think about the whole thing, we need to too. We cannot engineer our missile effectively if we don't know how finance is building their finance missile. Our missile system becomes ineffective because we are treating each one like a different product—when in fact, the whole system is the product.

Sector silos act more like agricultural silos. If you think about agricultural silos, you think of millions of little pieces of the exact same thing stuck in a single space, without access to the outside world. It's like a fish in a fishbowl—without any context that their fishbowl is in an apartment within a building within a city within the planet Earth. Silos limit our vision to see the world for what it really is. When all we can see is more grain, we might miss out on the fact that a woodchip in the next silo over might have the answer to, or actually solve, the problem. And the woodchip misses out on the grain.

There is power in putting yourself out where others wouldn't expect to see you. Consider a LinkedIn post from a corporate vice president asking for nonprofit leaders they can speak to in order to learn about their experiences working in corporate partnerships. A nonprofit leader getting an MBA and diving into the most corporate-focused curricula. Or a public servant moving from booth to booth at a conference on corporate leadership, noting that they are there to gain a better understanding of how businesses think about working with governments. This is the beauty of intersection work. You have no choice but to travel to distant sectors of space with your lifelong learner's hat squarely on your head.

Earlier in our book, we referenced mathematician and philosopher Antanas Mockus, mayor of Bogotá, Columbia, from 1995 to 1997 and again from 2001 to 2003, as a movement leader. Before he was established as such, early in his quest to end traffic fatalities, he beautifully demonstrated the results of acting like a network in getting out of your silo. Mockus brought not only a unique background to his job but also a unique approach. To him, teaching people to understand how a system worked was not enough. He believed people needed to directly teach one another. They could model better choices to inspire new ways of thinking in others. They could act like a network.

In trying to understand how people perceived the poor, potentially life-ending decisions they made to step into traffic, he brought in an ingenious group of thinkers who practiced in thinking about how human beings negotiate physical space. He hired a team of mimes. Those mimes shadowed pedestrians who did not obey the traffic signals, not unexpectedly to frequently hilarious results for onlookers. They did the same for the drivers. What started with just 20 silent employees physically demonstrating what not to do expanded to a program with 400 more citizens trained to be mime traffic cops.[1] Not quite what you expected to hear from a public official, even one clearly dedicated to building a movement, huh?

For most of us, physical travel is the answer to opening our minds to understanding how our perspective is limiting our view of the world. That's impractical and sometimes impossible for most of us, though. So here, we'll walk you through getting out of your professional silo and sector box while never leaving your office chair. Professional silos are also typically cultural silos. Even among large international teams, there is a dominant culture at play, typically from wherever the institution is based. At an intersection, the dominant culture shouldn't be based on one partner. Instead, the culture should be set by an equal influence of all the partners.

 Practicing getting out of your silo

To break down silos, Erin Meyer's *The Culture Map* is about as mind opening of a read as you can have to prepare for your work.[2] Remember how earlier we noted that Americans, in particular, are obsessed with the idea

continued

of singular brilliance? A professor at INSEAD, Meyer has identified eight different scales by which to understand differences in interactions between cultures. Many of these scales can be found elsewhere or originated with another's research, but she brought them together to tell a complete story. Looking for and noticing these will give you amazing practice for any attempt to shift your perspective. As you review these, try to guess where your culture falls on these scales. Start with your nationality, but perhaps go back through and think about your sector and specialization too.

1. *Low context vs. high context:* communication is expressed simply and understood to mean what it is offered at face value vs. communication is nuanced and understood to be read between the lines

2. *Direct negative feedback vs. indirect negative feedback:* blunt and honest feedback vs. diplomatic feedback, where negative messages are wrapped in positive ones

3. *Applications-first persuasion vs. principles-first persuasion:* begin with the fact or opinion and avoid theoretical discussions in a business environment vs. begin with a theoretical argument before offering a conclusion

4. *Egalitarian leadership vs. hierarchical leadership:* the best boss is a facilitator and has a short distance to their team vs. the best boss is a strong director and is to be communicated with along clear organizational structure lines

5. *Consensus decisions vs. top-down decisions:* decisions are made in groups vs. decisions are made by individuals

6. *Task-based trust vs. relationship-based trust:* trust is built through work activities and relationships are based on practical situations vs. trust is built through nonwork activities and relationships are deep and personal

7. *Confrontational disagreement vs. confrontation avoidance:*
debate and open confrontation are positive and won't nega-
tively impact relationships vs. debate and open confrontation
are negative and destructive to the group and so are avoided

8. *Linear-time scheduling vs. flexible-time scheduling:* sequential
approach to tasks with a focus on sticking to a schedule vs.
fluid approach to tasks and acceptance of interruptions as
opportunities arise

For example, Americans are likely to say that for decisions, they are a
consensus culture, but Meyer finds that not to be the case. Americans
fall squarely in the middle of the cultures she studied. Northern European
countries like the Netherlands, Germany, and Sweden would find it incredible for a boss to end a discussion with a statement like "This is what we are
going to do" and for employees to just go along with it, yet that happens
frequently in American companies. Seeing others' perspective of yourself
is eye opening. Working through this exercise, you may find you don't fall
on these scales where you think you do.

What Meyer doesn't go deeply into, however, is that these same scales
can frequently be applied between generations of workers, sectors, or
specializations. A Silicon Valley entrepreneur and a Wall Street banker are
likely to be heavily divided on these scales, regardless of what nationality
they are. These scales should be utilized first and foremost to identify
where you fall on the continuum and recognize that your collaborators
will likely fall further to one side or another. You can start practicing this
just in your office, thinking through how the people you work closest
to may differ from you. This can eventually also be a great exercise to
explore with your closest collaborators at an intersection, should they be
willing. There are other formal tools like this that read personalities, but

that is on a person-by-person level. At an intersection, you are seeking to understand entire organization or sector cultures different from yours.

In your silo, you are likely just surrounded by more pieces of grain like yourself. But even pieces of grain have unique differences when you look at them thoroughly enough. It is a great place to start, and your ability to be aware of these differences will serve you greatly when you get out of your silo. You will have to honestly and openly assess the opportunities available in your life to join spaces in which you can leap to another silo for a bit to practice further. Go back to the "not-work" list you created in chapter 6 and add something that you think will give you an opportunity to explore different cultures—national cultures, professional cultures, or otherwise. Or go back to your netstorming exercise in chapter 13 and expand on the list of connections you want to make. When combined with the skill in the next chapter, you'll be able to bridge communication divides.

CHAPTER 16

Learning Other Professional Languages

. . . .

The Culture Map also reinforces the idea that *everyone* is responsible for working together when cultural differences are at play. As someone trying to convene an intersection project, where consensus must be achieved, you can't expect people to suddenly accept a different approach from their deep-seated personal one. In the cases of consensus gathering, specifically when working with top-down cultures not used to that style, Meyer suggests gaining feedback and trying to build a shared view while striving to make decisions more quickly than usual in a consensus approach. The speed of decision-making will at least feel somewhat familiar to those from top-down cultures. This can keep a sense of respect for your authority, which top-down cultures lean toward, in the very act of you trying to build a shared authority, which consensus cultures lean toward. In other words, you have to give a little to get a little.

To build a shared vision, everyone must first understand one another's visions and speak one another's *professional* languages. People with similar professional and personal backgrounds tend to speak among themselves in shorthand, otherwise known as jargon, to ease communication. You only have to spend a little time in a hospital, airport, or commercial kitchen to see this in action. Jargon isn't necessarily a bad thing; it simplifies communication within a group of people who share an understanding of the concepts and ideas behind it. But to act like a network, you'll need to look beyond yourself and speak the professional language of your collaborators. Doing so demonstrates an understanding of their work and builds profound trust. It's hard to get others to share if you don't speak their language. For example, we've learned that speaking with engineers often requires a different language than speaking with marketing leaders. The same is true when you speak to a board of directors versus community activists. Speaking in someone else's professional language is a skill that is rooted in perspective and empathy. It involves realizing that you and your organization have certain norms, expectations, and approaches, and that while these are real and present for you and your organization, your partners and collaborators may have completely different norms, expectations, and approaches. Hopefully, in practicing the skills we've already discussed, you've started better understanding what they are.

 Practicing learning other professional languages

Language is vital. It frames our world, and the more of them you know, the better you are at accomplishing the shared work. Learning your partners' languages involves listening that helps you understand their perspective but then takes a step further to integrate the words, practices, and approaches used by others into your own speech. One of the most effective ways to gain insights into your partners' languages is to work with them in the same physical location, if only for a time. Much work and insight take place in the break room, at the watercooler, and at the copier. If you can, spend a week, a month, or a year co-working with your colleagues from other sectors. Magic can come from this time you spend together.

If you can't work in the same physical space for whatever reason, you can still learn their language. A technique frequently taught in interview workshops is mirroring. The general idea is that to win the favor of some-one, you subtly project physical similarity to them. If they lean forward in their chair, you lean forward. If they begin the conversation by mak-ing small talk with a few simple questions, you return the favor. This will not get you nearly as deep as colocating, but this can be done on video calls and in text communications. It's similar to speaking a basic, broken version of language to a native speaker: it may not have been perfect, but your message got through and the native speaker appreciated your efforts. Your attempt to even try touches heartstrings. In some small but vital way, you are earnestly trying to be inside their world.

And you can expand this technique. Next time, don't just mirror but also try to feel how the way you copy their actions influences your perception of their world. When you lean forward because they do, do you feel a deeper sense of intimacy or intention? When you engage in the small talk because they do, do you feel the slight tinge of discomfort and distance it creates, or perhaps do you sense yourself trying to put them at ease? Perhaps you feel both simultaneously. What does how they deliver their language say about their perspective of the world?

Returning to Meyer and *The Culture Map*, while there are clear ben-efits to be gained from learning another professional language, there is also a cost. Misunderstandings that can be easily avoided can feel deeply personal and derailing. In other words, this is low-effort, high-impact stuff to pay attention to. For instance, Americans do not like to give or receive direct criticism. A German person may tell it to them direct, expecting it to be taken as a stern but not forceful critique—and find the American person shaking nervously the next day, unable to concentrate at work. Or an American person might try to kindly point out "just one little thing" to a German about their work, and the German person will walk away feeling they are knocking it out of the park, because only one small thing was wrong. They may never change their behavior, and the tension will eventually erupt.

The truth is, we all learn other languages every moment of our lives. We are willing to bet your use of emojis was way better in 2023 than in 2013. When you start a new job, it doesn't take long to throw out insider acronyms as if you've been doing it your whole life. More simply, the moment you meet a new person and interact with them, their language and physical mannerisms are now on the table for your vocabulary. If you ever laugh that you and your best friend sound the same, that's because you've learned each other's languages to a level of complete mastery. All we are suggesting is becoming attuned to this phenomenon. At a real-life intersection, say at a four-way stop, when we look left and right, we are not just looking for oncoming cars. We are also instantly evaluating behaviors, noticing the speed at which someone is braking or the focus of the person approaching the crosswalk, and making assumptions about upcoming choices as a result. We are all incredibly practiced at this, thanks to learning our technical skills and recognizing our innate intuition. Becoming attuned and observational to the ways you and others connect to the world will transport you from the silo behind your wheel to what it feels like to sit behind their wheel. Perhaps you will have a little less road rage!

Learning your partners' languages helps you understand their perspective and, in turn, broadens your own. It is only after you have seen things from new, sometimes disorienting vantage points that you can truly recognize the solid ground you are sharing with those around you. Seeing the world with fresh eyes, taking that Matrix pill, allows you to act on the reality that you are not the only person who needs their vision to be shared in this scenario. The next step is to connect the wires of your brain with everyone else's, creating the "brain" of the partnership. We'll use code-switching and, ultimately, code-mixing to do that.

CHAPTER 17

Building the Future on Public Land

· ·

At the northern tip of the "City by the Bay" lies one of the most stunning pieces of land in North America. Home to the Ohlone Native people for centuries, the land now known as the Presidio of San Francisco served many uses over recent years, mostly militarily. With the arrival of the New Deal programs, World Wars, and the concurrent growth of the US military in the first half of the 20th century, the Presidio saw a significant buildup, including investment in hospitals, major housing complexes, and the addition of the Crissy Field airstrip. In the same era, the construction of the Golden Gate Bridge also played an important part in the Presidio's infrastructure since the south anchorages and approaches are located on Presidio land.

Like many military bases, the Presidio became outdated when its lands and infrastructure were no longer needed for strategic military interests. On approximately 1,500 acres of land, the Presidio housed over 870 buildings and structures, some dating back to the US Civil War era. In 1994, this was deemed to be excess to the army and the land was transferred to the National Park Service (NPS).[1] The NPS is best known for managing large tracts of natural resource intensive parks like Yosemite, Yellowstone, or Grand Canyon. Of course, these parks also have significant human-built infrastructure to support visitors. While it can't compete with the army, the NPS nevertheless has substantial resources—it is a multimillion-dollar federal agency with tens of thousands of employees. Still, many in Congress and the local community were concerned that the federal government couldn't allocate NPS the necessary resources to manage a sprawling former military reservation. They also worried that the rest of the national park system would suffer greatly if substantial resources were allocated to manage a national park in an urban area like the Presidio. Further, prominent members of Congress questioned whether the US government should provide taxpayer funds to support a park in such an expensive urban area. Many fiscally conservative members wondered whether it made more sense to sell the park's vast real estate assets to pay off the federal deficit.

A long and complicated political battle ensued that, like many things political, resulted in a grand compromise—the idea of forming the nation's first and only self-supporting national park.[2] Many were concerned that the idea would at best fail and at worst set a precedent whereby the government would expect other national parks to be self-sustaining, thus ushering in an era of disinvestment in parks. Congress ultimately decided to provide initial funding for 15 years and then require self-sufficiency moving forward. The legislation stipulated that if self-sufficiency wasn't achieved, the vast real estate and land holdings of the Presidio would be sold as excess US government property, likely ushering in commercial development of previously protected property.

A fierce debate followed about what would happen to the Presidio. Could a national park actually become financially self-sufficient? Would the NPS have the capacity and skills to manage a tract of land that was so different from the majority of its other responsibilities? Would the NPS have the business skills to create a self-sufficient park? What would happen to these treasured lands, and what would San Francisco look like if these lands were developed? The debate became personal and ugly at times as politicians and constituents felt the weight of the future of San

Francisco and public lands in their laps. Further, the NPS itself felt as if its competence and its mission were under question and threat.

The solution involved many months of hard work, lobbying, community meetings, and political wrangling. A new organization was formed, a wholly owned government corporation with a self-sufficiency mandate called the Presidio Trust. The Trust is a hybrid organization—it acts in part like a national park and in part like a real estate rental and development company. Legally it is a government agency, and it oversees many traditional park management and preservation functions over a vast collection of historic buildings and sensitive park lands. However, it also has broader borrowing and leasing authorities than most other government agencies, employees lack typical civil service protections, and the director reports to a board of directors appointed by the president of the United States, rather than through the NPS system. Most parks are supported by federal appropriations, and yet, due to the vast real estate assets in the former military base, many believed that the Trust could become self-supporting through leasing the assets. Simply put, the Trust had the potential to change the traditional model of national parks in the United States. And many would argue, it did just that.

The lessons of the Trust's success are many—indeed numerous authors have written about the topic.[3] Noteworthy to us is that the success of the Trust exemplifies the skills of *Act Like a Network* we have dissected to this point, specifically the skills of *Getting Out of Your Silo*, *Acting as Part of a Whole*, and *Learning Other Professional Languages*.

Getting out of your silo

The leaders working to make the Presidio Trust a reality believed that they needed to get outside the silo of park-based models and scour the country for case studies of different kinds of sites that provided a relevant background for the formation of the Trust. The team turned to the venerable consulting firm McKinsey and Company, which agreed to take on the project on a pro bono basis. They assigned a team of consultants to the project who analyzed 19 models of public/private/governmental partnerships that could serve as models for the Presidio. Most of the models studied by McKinsey were not park-based models. Of the 19 models the consultants studied, only eight were NPS sites. The consultants drew their findings from a wide array of partnerships that had the potential to act as examples for the new network for the Presidio. For example, the McKinsey team studied the Pennsylvania Avenue Development Corporation, which was responsible for redeveloping much of the area around the White House in Washington, DC. From this model, the consultants drew important ideas about ways in which private developers, leasing experts, and nontraditional financing sources could be brought into the network and what approaches could be utilized in the effort to make the Presidio self-sufficient.

Many believe that this approach of looking outside national park–based models was essential to the success of the Trust. Prior to the publication of McKinsey's findings, the discourse was limited—should the NPS manage the Presidio or not? Following publication, the conversation broadened significantly to focus on what skills were needed to make the Presidio a success and how those skills should be deployed and by whom. It was these recommendations that helped the leaders working to design the Presidio's governing organization to create successful operational structures and pave the way to creative financing, real estate leasing, and new models for national parks that ultimately led to the Presidio's success.

Acting as a part of a whole

The leaders working on the Presidio transformation saw it as much more than a national park site—they saw it as a cultural treasure important to the very soul of the country. They wanted to rise above the bickering between NPS officials, neighbors, and the City of San Francisco and elevate the conversation. They saw the Trust as part of a whole of cultural institutions in the United States, much like the venerable Smithsonian museums, Pearl Harbor, or Metropolitan Opera.

As a result, they convened an influential group of civic and corporate leaders called the Presidio Council. The Presidio Council was active in lobbying to save the Presidio, researching models to ensure the sustainability and protection of the Presidio, and securing funds to pay staff and lobbyist costs. The Presidio Council included CEOs of major corporations, leaders of museums and cultural institutions, and executive directors of major environmental organizations. The Presidio Council also had a small paid staff that included a consultant responsible for lobbying and keeping track of key legislation regarding the Presidio. The group had deep political and social connections—they had access that allowed them to influence policy in both California and Washington, DC. Perhaps equally importantly, they had credibility in a variety of spheres because they were leaders from multiple sectors. Especially noteworthy in the composition of the Presidio Council is that it comprised artists like Maya Lin (designer of the Vietnam Veterans Memorial), activists like Carl Anthony of the Urban Habitat Institute, and environmental and park leaders. Talk about getting many boats in the water!

The members of the Presidio Council broadened the network of support to save the Presidio and shifted the conversation to an entirely new level. The group helped others see that the Presidio was much more significant than many perceived. They elevated it from a regional concern in the San Francisco area to being part of a whole movement of preserving cultural institutions. They moved the conversation away from discussing the Presidio as just one of hundreds of national park sites to viewing it as an iconic American place. This shift in attention changed Congress's attention and helped the Presidio gain important legislative authorizations that helped it succeed. The Presidio Trust was born and became the hybrid organization to care for the Presidio and ensure its financial and environmental sustainability and its rightful place in American environmental and historical preservation.

Learning other professional languages

The Trust, first and foremost, is an organization charged with preserving and enhancing irreplaceable natural and cultural treasures. Like most national parks, the Trust employs hundreds of park professionals, rangers, natural and cultural resource experts, and the like. And yet the Trust deeply understands and practices the professional language of real estate. The Trust employs hundreds of real estate professionals—people who restore, fix, transform, and lease real estate. In this way, the Trust is not unlike many real estate companies. Their professionals plan, finance, improve, transform, and lease historic buildings at market rates. They also partner extensively with commercial real estate brokers, and their hundreds of units of residential property are comanaged with residential leasers. The revenue from this leasing and real estate activity is at the core of what makes the Trust self-sustaining.

There are, of course, occasional tensions between the real estate and park functions of the Trust. The important lesson is that both professional languages exist in the organization. Traditionally parks and real estate were at odds. The Trust has bridged the gap and helped people realize that both are essential to the Presidio. The park building functions are supported by the real estate leasing. And, of course, the reason that people want to live and work in the Presidio is because of its unique park attributes. These tensions, and the work done to get through them, set us up perfectly to introduce our next skill, *Code-Mixing with Intention*.

Conclusion

Despite the controversies, most would say that today the Trust is a success—it reached its self-sufficiency goal ahead of schedule and restored hundreds of buildings and many acres of parkland. The Presidio is transformed. It is a stunning place to recreate, adventure, and enjoy an unparalleled park experience. It preserves sensitive species and habitat and tells the stories of several centuries of history. And it does this at little or no cost to the federal taxpayer.

A visit to the Presidio is always memorable, and we hope this inspires you to make the trip. It is a constant reminder of years of important history. It welcomes us to pause and reflect. Simultaneously, the Presidio shows us the power of what happens when we act like a network.

CHAPTER 18

Code-Mixing with Intention

. . . .

Once you learn languages, which language you use in what situation, when, and with whom becomes an extremely important choice. In other words, code-switching—when we act one way with one group and a different way with a different group. Code-switching is a skill worth developing in its own right, but it's especially useful in intersection work.

We may, often unconsciously, switch the tenor, approach, or style of the words we're using depending on the people we're with. The comedy duo Key and Peele famously parodied the way President Obama openly code-switched as he would make his way down a line shaking hands at an event, bringing a much more familial and affectionate tone to his inter-actions with Black attendees than white attendees.[1] There are also, sadly, many who feel forced to code-switch in ways that do not feel comfort-able. Films like *Sorry to Bother You* (2018) and *BlacKkKlansman* (2018) bring more disturbing comedic looks at the troubling elements of what access you gain when you "sound white." Code-switching can sometimes feel inauthentic or forced to succeed in a world that doesn't feel as if it welcomes you. Much can be gained, however, in moments where you can still be genuine to who you are and show an understanding of your partners without losing yourself or becoming fake.

Code-switching is often used by leaders as they work with different cultures or subcultures in an organization in a way that can still maintain, and in fact demands, authenticity. Code-switching takes mirroring one step further as a form of cultural communication—you choose to actually adopt some of the cultural norms of a colleague, particularly when working with them. If you come from a more confrontational culture, perhaps with certain colleagues you become less confrontational to fit their cultural norms. Perhaps you give more direct feedback to an employee who responds better to that. Or you adopt informal communication with a boss who prefers that approach. We likely already, often unconsciously, switch approach or style of the words we're using depending on the people we're with. The best way to use code-switching skills authentically, of course, is to consciously spend time immersing yourself in the work of the subcultures of the organizations you're hoping to influence, especially if you're not traditionally experienced in these disciplines.

It is perhaps here where the oft interchanged or overlooked but subtly different concept of code-mixing comes into play. Code-mixing generally refers to speaking in a combination of multiple languages and using words and grammatical elements from numerous sources at once to guide the conversation when needed. It allows you to speak to engineers and marketing leaders at the same time in a combination of their languages. Marketing wants to sell more things; engineers want to make good things. What do they have in common? Often customer usability is one place they can meet. More and more companies insert engineers into the product design process early—the room comes alive as the product is looked at from every angle, and you end up with something you can build *and* sell.

You can see how this works in real life with Spanglish, a mix of English and Spanish. Spanglish may be practiced in certain situations out of necessity to sound a certain way (before President Obama was parodied for his code-switching after all, President George W. Bush was parodied for his not-always-successful attempts to speak Spanish), but at its root, it simply is just a manner of communication for people who have grown up with both language influences. It has become a code-mixed language of its own right, with each culture behind the languages reflected and combined to create a whole new vocabulary.

At the very least, as it often did politically for President Bush, code-mixing goes a long way to earning trust. Just as reading a book like *The Culture Map* might prepare you for international differences in communication practices, so too would calling on your network for understanding how corporations, nonprofits, and public-sector institutions differ in their cultural approaches. It probably doesn't take a big leap to guess at some of the differences in style and approach to expect. You don't have to have stepped foot in Silicon Valley, for instance, to know that dressing more casually than you would at a big accounting firm, quickly shifting to a first-name basis, and talking about your outside-of-work explorations is the norm.

This, however, is why code-mixing is so important to separate from code-switching. By code-mixing, you're trying to help others understand that you are open to learning and growing from their perspectives and equally inviting them to learn and grow from yours. In an intersection environment, code-switching might build comfort with one another's languages, but code-mixing allows you to co-create a shared language. Intersections are an opportunity to find common ground. Perhaps you still wear your suit in Silicon Valley, but you wear a tie that speaks to the more casual and adventurous part of you. You mix your language with theirs. You bring your authentic self and invite them to do so as well. To attempt to do so without losing yourself and the codes by which you operate will engender an important mix of gratitude and respect. It is the ultimate truth behind the "just be yourself" guidance we all cringed at when we were teenagers. Because it's actually not just about being you: it's also about recognizing and accepting the others waiting at the intersection. Your Spanish and their English might combine to become your shared Spanglish. This is the only way to build a system we can all agree on. It must be one we can all authentically see ourselves reflected in as unique voices but also see as a cohesive whole.

Code-mixing is an invitation to feel just a little more comfortable, seen, and recognized while recognizing that other languages and ways of seeing the world are valid. It is an invitation to present one's worthy ideas and to listen to others' too. It allows everyone, even in a small way, to see themselves in you. And that engenders trust. Without trust, diversity in the workplace is meaningless. Diversity brings conflicting opinions of how to see the world and how to do work. The result is a stronger product that will appeal across sectors. Across silos. But if people don't trust that when they speak their mind, offer their different opinion, it will be heard, then all you have is something that looks good on the corporate brochure.

 Practicing code-mixing with intention

Acting like a network speaks louder than words. But our words have power. We recommend you keep a running list of words that you hear your collaborators bringing to the table that are different or specific to their sectors. Add your own words. Begin a co-created language and start using it. Your initiation will be a subconscious invitation. When the time is right, you can even recommend hosting a shared dictionary of terms that all can access. If you are handy with a PowerPoint, a simple Venn diagram can take it one step further. This can demonstrate to your partners perhaps what words or work styles seem to be overlapping and which ones to perhaps be careful of. This can be another page to your "intersection dictionary."

Of course, code-mixing cannot be earned cheaply. It takes time—people create dictionaries after language is naturally created. You can't let the dictionary dictate what is allowed to be said and what is not. You run the risk of people simply code-switching to your "code-mixed" language in the room and then reverting to their original language silos outside the room, complaining that their true opinions aren't heard and that this co-created language is just diluting all sides. All of this is a risk. But as we will discuss in an ensuing chapter, the reward can be worth the risk.

CHAPTER 19

Understanding Hidden Power

. . . .

By definition, much work in public-private partnerships is accomplished with government partners. Government partners often have very specific legal authorizations and authorities within which they work. These legal authorities are usually granted by the federal, state, or local body. As a result, much of what takes place at an intersection is ultimately related to regulations, political decisions, and political influence. The government agency usually can't legally change the authority, but often the partners have the ability to influence lawmakers to change the authorizations. Gaining these authorizations and managing the bureaucratic landscape is a skill unto itself for complex intersection partnerships. Not unlike knowing how to code software for a computer start-up, understanding the operating system and approach of the government is essential.

In our research, we were struck by the critical gatekeeping roles staffers, assistants, schedulers, and even sometimes door attendants have for powerful government leaders. Most politicians are moving so quickly that they can barely keep up with even the most basic details. They depend on their gatekeepers to manage critical pieces of information and access. If you want to accomplish important work to affect policy and outcomes, working with the hidden power structure is essential. Once structures are uncovered, organizational leaders need to put a lot of time and energy into framing, or reframing, the narrative. To act like a network, you will also need to access critical information from the people getting the tasks done. They also know who else is getting tasks done and often have their own networks they've tapped into. And this is not just found in governments. This should feel pretty familiar to anyone who has ever had an innovative idea, only to see it somehow swallowed by a hidden force before it ever got started.

But how do you see what you're not seeing? The first step is to simply understand how hidden power works.

We don't consciously think about the effect of politics in systems outside the government, yet they're still at play. We need to see who has power, who doesn't, and how we can influence the outcome. An ADP Research Institute study in 2019 set out to understand employee engagement, capturing 1,000 participants from 19 different countries.[1] One of the more stunning responses it revealed was that over 50 percent of workers identified being part of a team that was not represented on their organizational chart. Commenting on the study in a 2019 *Harvard Business Review* article, Marcus Buckingham and Ashley Goodall wittily noted that "if a manager wants to formally add someone to his or her team, that manager has to call up HR and ask permission to move a 'head count' (which basically means a paycheck) from one box to another. Approvals have to be applied for, budgets have to be consulted, permissions must be granted up and down the chain, until finally white smoke appears from the chimney and lo and behold, the new head count appears in a new box on the org chart."[2]

The reality, of course, is that teams simply emerge to get work done. It pains us to say this as consultants who are often brought in to build formal structures around teams, but if you want people to work together well, often the best medicine is to simply allow them to socialize and find one another naturally. It is easy to posit that perhaps the most efficient and powerful teams are those that go around the bureaucratic rules that would slow them down. Without formal rules that can be imposed to stop or shape their interactions, they are hard to put into check. In corporations, sadly, instead of being provided support from organizations to leverage the energy they maintain, they are often, at best, sidelined or, at worst, pressured to dismantle. This creates a hidden challenge for intersection work. It's hard enough to find partners to collaborate with, but it's nearly impossible if you can't even see who the people are who you truly need to win over to your side.

Practicing understanding hidden power

One way to understand hidden power is to create a simple diagram where you plot the various entities involved in an initiative or issue you're working on. In our work, we use a chart to gain a quick but surprisingly informative look at where we should be paying attention in order to solve a problem. In this case, the y-axis should represent the degree of perceived power of the entities in your issue area, and the x-axis should represent the degree of interest the players in those entities have in the initiative or issue area.

continued

One great example we've seen comes from a power versus interest graph created by a group of researchers working with workshop participants on a food systems change initiative (see the graph at the beginning of this section).[3] The workshop participants identified 34 stakeholder groups with interest in that topic that their initiative was attempting to influence. A simple diagram like this can yield important insights about power and focus for your network-building activities. For example, the diagram reveals that the initiative may want to focus on network-building activities with logistics firms, consumers, and legislators since these three groups have both high power and high interest in the topic. Likewise, the initiative might want to spend less time focusing on network building with lobbyists (high power but low interest) or health care providers (high interest but low power).

As you likely know, the backroom dealings of Washington actually have a lot in common with the cluster of cubicles in an office building. They are both, in many ways, where the true power lies. To find that power, consider creating a "social network analysis" chart for an initiative you're working on. Start by analyzing emails and other team communications for who is included in the communications (especially people who aren't directly involved) and who gives credit to whom. Observe in meetings who went over to whom during a break. And, if possible, ask your organizational partners who the people are who really get things done.

Draw lines connecting those people who get things done to those in power. Much like the network map we introduced in chapter 13, soon your orderly chart will look like a chart of all the stars in the sky.

Important stories will emerge from activities like these. Who is at the hub of the network? That is, who has the most lines connecting them to others or sits at the farthest top-right corner of perceived power and interest? Global leadership expert and Babson College professor Rob Cross and consultant Lawrence Prusak identified four types of people to specifically look for in a social network analysis map. They called the ones with the most connections, aptly, "central connectors." They also identified "boundary spanners," whose lines go the longest, hopping across departments or even organizations to people outside their silo. "Information brokers" sit at the edges of clusters, creating a direct connection with another critical group or two. Finally, "peripheral specialists" sit at the edge as people whom you can turn to for un-intrenched opinions and expertise.[4]

And who is the person who holds the keys to you getting to the hub, the one with the line from the hub that eventually reaches you? From there, put your courage to the sticking place and interject yourself into the informal interactions with the network line that will eventually gain you the ear of the person with access to the hub you're trying to reach. This is especially important because so much leverageable power is completely hidden. For example, lobbyists are working with political staffers to write legislation that can make your work succeed or fail. If you don't have the resources to counter their lobbying power, then you need to rely on your networks. By working with your networks, you may have even more power over those who have formal power.

We didn't say this was going to be easy. But like many things, awareness is the first step. The goal is to expose what's hidden. In doing so, you may just find yourself starting to be seen as the leader among the partners, beginning to build a more powerful network for change and rally people together to build . . . a movement.

Our final skill for *Act Like a Network* sets you up to begin to lead like a movement. It is the gateway to transform your ability from getting boats in the water to pointing them in the right direction as a unified fleet. Not surprisingly, it's about encouraging people to think differently and rewarding them when they do so.

CHAPTER 20

Rewarding Risk

· ·

As humans, we have an odd relationship with risk. We try to minimize risk in much of our everyday lives, and yet study after study tells us that we often worry about the wrong risk. We're worrying about rare risks, like plane crashes and earthquakes, and minimizing the far more common risks, like car accidents when we drive daily.

We should be emulating how entrepreneurs take risks. While we often hear that entrepreneurs are great risk-takers, in actuality most successful entrepreneurs are extremely careful with managing risk. They take small, calculated risks at the beginning of projects as they learn about the work. They apply what they learn to the next risks they take, gradually taking bigger risks but backing them up with recent lessons. We can learn much by taking lots of small risks and observing the results. When we venture away from the known, we need to reframe our "failures" as learning and experimentation. This is essential in intersection work, because we're trying new approaches and we're going to have many moments where things don't go as planned. But we learn. That's the point. If we want things to go differently, we must try new approaches.

As a leader working at the intersection, you need to reward yourself and others for taking smaller risks as learning opportunities. As one rather memorable tactic, in 2012, CEO of Extended Stay America Jim Donald handed out a batch of "Get Out of Jail Free" cards from

Monopoly to his employees.[1] The company had recently returned from bankruptcy, and tensions were understandably high. Employees seemed to feel that any failure could lead to struggles for the company or, worse, losing their jobs. Donald, the former CEO of Starbucks, itself one of the more innovative, risk-taking companies in the world, recognized that this tendency to avoid taking calculated risks could mean death in times of financial challenge. Whenever an employee wanted to take a big risk, they handed in their card. It helped embolden employees. For example, when a rumor circulated that a certain film might be coming to town for an on-location shoot, one employee cold-called the producers and ended up with a $250,000 group booking.[2] This is what comes from rewarding risk. Not only did the small risk reap a large financial payout, but the risk also significantly built the network out to hundreds of new contacts who now became ambassadors for the brand.

Donald is far from alone. In fact, a number of corporations have begun to reward employees for, of all things, failure. They allow space for ideas that might not only get us to our goals but also rewrite our goals into something we hadn't dreamed of. When everyone is excited about a new thing, then there is no need to find halfway agreements about the old thing. If you have ever been in a room where excitement toward a plan of action is palpable, it is likely it was because the idea was not expected, and it came from what was perceived as an unlikely source. Such situations don't happen by accident; they often come from taking a small risk of being embarrassed by proposing something, which builds momentum to something completely fresh.

The First Penguin Award was first established by Dr. Randy Pausch, a computer science professor at Carnegie Mellon University, and captured the concept of rewarding risk in his book *The Last Lecture*.[3] Penguins, like many wild animals, survive because personal risk is undertaken for the good of the group. Penguins line up to dive into the sea to hunt for food, without any knowledge of what hunters lie below. The first penguin, therefore, has a high potential of failure and literally puts itself in harm's way for the sake of exploration. The rest of the group is relieved. Even if the penguin's individual actions were unnecessary, somebody had to shake up the current goal of marching across ice sheets, or else they would have starved. A new goal of finding fish in the water is put in play, and it turns out penguins are pretty great swimmers and hunters. The leap of faith was worth the risk.

Pausch used this award in his "Building Virtual Worlds" class, bestowing it to teams whose big ideas or engineering of new technologies ultimately failed. What he described as a "glorious failure" was applauded by winners who "were losers who were definitely going somewhere."[4] Because unlike penguins, humans typically survive their first failure and learn and grow from it. "All life is an experiment," Ralph Waldo Emerson once said. "The more experiments you make the better." And you don't need to be a CEO or a classroom teacher to do this. Nothing is stopping you from giving someone a prize for failure.

Truly, the only thing really standing in your way from being able to reward risk and support other voices is learning to take risks yourself. It is what gives you the authority, and, indeed, the hidden power, to command respect from the non-risk-takers in the room. As the old adage goes, true leaders lead by example.

 Practicing rewarding risk

Not so comfortable with risk? Many of us aren't. Start small and work your way to bigger risks:

1. Begin with a risk whose failure only you can see and has limited consequence to you. Learn that you survive.

2. Expose yourself to a risk that could be seen by someone but will not likely affect anyone, including yourself. Realize that

continued

any public shame is lessened once you can name it. It ceases to be some imperceivable mass of possibilities.

3. Move on to a risk that has a minor consequence to yourself.

4. Take a risk that has a minor consequence to yourself and others.

These risks can be anything. Don't think you have a good sense of humor? Here's what you can do:

1. Don't fake-laugh at a joke you don't understand.

2. Tell a joke you have seen someone else tell successfully.

3. Tell a joke that you think is funny but haven't seen anyone deliver successfully.

4. Ask a friend to tell that same joke for you and see if they can deliver it successfully. Make sure they promise to tell everyone that it was your joke afterward.

In other words, treat taking risks like something you can learn to do. It's truly that simple. If you recognize that you will survive the fall, then the next time you may jump off a slightly bigger cliff.

One way of learning to take work-related risks is to get your ideas out early and often. In our work, we've created a culture that helps people feel safe in presenting their work in a messy first draft that we share internally (but never with clients). It helps make it OK to err in the spirit of overcoming perfectionism. As a result, our work often advances further and faster. Taking the first step of writing your ideas down is often the hardest. When ideas are in your head, you can fool yourself into thinking that they're feasible. Once you write them down, you can start to see the holes in your approach. Getting the ideas out of your head actually helps you think deeper and refine them more. Plus, you're one step closer to getting the input and advice of others.

Your goal is to take small risks early and often. Andy Hargadon reminds us to make the $5 mistake before the $50, $500, $5,000, and $50,000 mistakes. In his workshops, Hargadon encourages participants to develop a short pitch deck for their ideas, print it out, and take a colleague out to a $5 coffee to get feedback. The rewards can be powerful. By getting your ideas into a presentation, you begin what Hargadon calls the "think-do," which moves you from taking small risks to learning from them to advancing your project. The think-do cycle encourages us to take risks in stages. Do some thinking, then take a risk. Evaluate the learning. Do more thinking and refining, and then take the next risk.

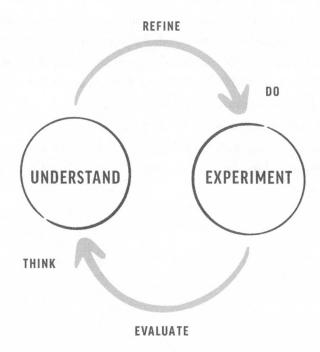

Think-do allows you and your partners to learn with lots of opportunity to refine. So often we overthink ideas before trying them out and taking the risk. A think-think-think-do can limit how much you can learn and how quickly. It also won't prepare you as well for eventual failures. It's much better to think-do lots of times, learning more, faster. You'll also build your new network in the process, because if you're comfortable with taking smaller risks more often, your partners at the intersection will become more comfortable with taking risks too. And when they see how you learn from your mistakes rather than giving up or blaming others, they'll trust you more.

Acting like a network ultimately comes down to one word: trust. You need to trust others enough to put yourself in the vulnerable position of learning their language and making mistakes in front of them. They need to trust you to be equally vulnerable to take their great penguin leap into the unknown icy waters below. And to gain that trust, for your partners, actions truly speak louder than words. Once you have made those efforts, an interesting thing will start happening. Whether you have formal authority or not, people will recognize your capability to empathize with them and help them bring the best out of themselves. In other words, they will start turning to you for leadership.

With that in mind, let's go once more to a case study that shows how acting like a network, utilizing the skills we've detailed in this section, aligned and inspired a movement in a perhaps unlikely place—city government.

CHAPTER 21

Driving Sustainability in Cities

· ·

According to the World Bank, more people now live in cities than in rural or suburban areas.[1] This is where most of us work, play, raise our families, and spend time. In North America, where local governmental entities lead each of our cities, it can be hard to create wide-scale sustainable change. Local governments are one of the most potent examples of silos we've discussed. The officials in New York City's government care about their city—same in Los Angeles, Orlando, Omaha, or any other city. And yet, there's so much that could be learned by one city from another about implementing initiatives, developing partnerships, securing funding, and measuring progress. State and federal governments can and do help see the bigger picture, but they also have their own silos that can make it hard to get on the same page.

Recognizing the need to accelerate action on sustainability issues and seeing the power of acting like a network to learn from one another, a group of local government leaders and partners founded the Urban Sustainability Directors Network (USDN) in 2008.[2] The goal in founding USDN was to share trusted information, build economies of scale, and create alignment and impact among the heads of traditional city environmental agencies, sustainability departments, or mayor's office or city council special initiatives. By 2022, this powerful network represented over 250 cities in North America with over 2,000 members who serve over 100 million residents.[3]

Act like a network

The formation of USDN embodies the idea of acting like a network; its structure and ways of operating reflect that goal. Acting like a network allowed USDN to create a small organization with an enormous reach. With fewer than 25 employees, USDN leverages the impact of thousands of members on behalf of millions of residents.

This network approach works because USDN requires its members to be actively involved in developing and maintaining the network. With many boats in the water, USDN can funnel and magnify the actions of its members to a much more significant impact. The USDN platform then becomes a great example of code-mixing with intention. Membership is only open to government staff with cross-departmental and community-wide responsibility for sustainability programs. To co-create a shared language that crosses geographic differences across the US (and Canada), USDN funnels activities into two main categories: peer learning and collaboration. You can easily replace these two terms with two others: mirroring and combining ideas.

Indeed, if you look at how USDN breaks down what collaboration means for the organization and its members, it's practically a step-by-step on how to code switch and, eventually, code mix. First, it asks its members to innovate "around shared challenges," building a space for members to switch their language from their local focus to a mutual focus. To do this, USDN encourages self-formed peer-to-peer user groups composed of members who openly share problems and challenges on a particular issue. Second, it recognizes that members end up "learning together as they adopt similar practices," the beginning of a co-creation or code-mixing of a language. To enable this, USDN sets up small group "marketplace" conversations between seven to ten members; agendas include short presentations and time for discussion. The result? USDN supports the third element of collaboration: for members to exert "their collective influence on the field."[4] USDN coordinates working groups of ten or more to co-create tools or products to address issues around field building such as professional development, innovation, regional networks, and public policy.

Unquestionably, one of the benefits of USDN's network approach is that it can help its members learn from one another before an individual city undertakes a new initiative. In effect, members can plan for potential obstacles they might not have otherwise anticipated. This can be particularly important in understanding hidden power. For example, one of the challenges facing cities in responding to climate change is building resilience in the city's infrastructure planning. A recent USDN report reminds its members that to build resilience into its planning, a city leader will likely need to work with no fewer than eight different city departments (health, emergency, planning, public works, housing, central services, transportation, and sustainability) to accomplish successful climate resilience work.[5] Each of these departments likely has its own goals and connections to city leadership. They all have hidden power that could scuttle the resilience efforts. USDN offers solutions learned from other cities' efforts to help manage this hidden power and move to a successful shared outcome.

Another example of the power of USDN acting like a network is its skill in getting out of its silo and learning other professional languages. USDN's staff has been critical in helping its members connect with and understand how foundation and corporate funders work. These are not typically skills developed well by government leaders. For example, in its early days, USDN created an Innovation Fund by partnering with foundations. Within five years of its founding, USDN was able to award over $700,000 to 18 collaborative projects.[6] Typically, collaborative projects involve three or more cities in the USDN network, so learning from the process and outcomes can be shared throughout the network. Further, by involving multiple cities in the projects, the collaborators can learn from one another and discover their own blind spots.

USDN's Innovation Fund allows its members to utilize another skill we uncovered in our research: rewarding risk. Government leaders face intense responsibility and scrutiny over the use of public funds, hindering innovation because the system creates incentives against risk and uncertainty. Yet we know that smart and appropriate risks are critical to innovation. Philanthropic funds don't face the same level of scrutiny as public funds. Thus, USDN's Innovation Fund allows its members to innovate and take calculated risks without fear of the same consequences for mistakes with taxpayers' money.

Lead like a movement

As USDN has grown and matured, it has increasingly started leading like a movement—an evolution that we, of course, applaud. Its recent strategic plan includes a pyramid-shaped diagram depicting the base of the pyramid as "network development," the middle layer as "practice advancement," and the top of the pyramid as "field leadership." The middle layer and especially the top layer, field leadership, are precisely what we mean by leading like a movement. USDN describes the services of field leadership it will provide as "field intelligence," "thought leadership," and "mobilization." For USDN, mobilization involves "focused opportunities to share knowledge and insight to influence policy and action at other levels of government."[7] This is movement leadership at its best. USDN is well poised to take the diverse cities in its network and point them in the same direction in powerful ways.

The next part of the book describes the skills involved in leading like a movement, such as building diversity, integrating multiple logics, and managing incumbents. USDN is a great model for us to learn from and emulate. For example, one of USDN's current strategies is to "develop and deploy opportunities to deepen partnerships between local governments and community-based organizations to maximize equity impacts of local action."[8] Given that its members serve cities with a collective population exceeding 100 million inhabitants, the results have the potential to be game changing for the movement to create a more sustainable future.

In late 2022, USDN received a $1.5 million grant from American Express to help some of its member cities install solar energy in low- to moderate-income homes and small businesses.[9] While corporate funding of environmental initiatives in the nonprofit sector isn't new, USDN is poised to help bridge the traditional lack of connection between corporations and investment in local government initiatives.

Conclusion

The devastating effects of climate change are becoming more and more evident and expensive. USDN is providing critical solutions to solve this crisis. Seeing how its approach may be transferrable to other entrenched problems is even more exciting to us. From its beginning, USDN acted like a network, and now it is translating this network into a massive force to lead like a movement on sustainability. It's fun to imagine what could happen if other organizations utilized similar approaches to solving global poverty, racial injustice, or any number of critical issues.

PART 3

LEAD LIKE A MOVEMENT

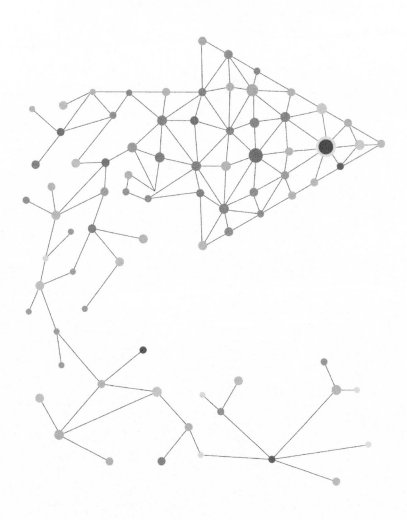

CHAPTER 22

Lead Like a Movement Overview

. . . .

As discussed in the last section, building a powerful, consciously designed network allows you to greatly broaden your vision for your work. Now you need to set the direction to allow the network to work effectively and coherently. As we noted in chapter 3, we're asking you to shift your approach and think of yourself as building a social movement for change so that you think about your project in a different light.

One of the misconceptions about social movement action is that it takes place spontaneously. Sometimes this happens, but more often movements are well planned and well executed. In this section, we'll cover the essentials of the planning and execution necessary to lead like a movement. First you must recruit a team with diverse perspectives, backgrounds, and lived experiences. Then you must bring together multiple logics and establish feedback loops to ensure those diverse perspectives are integrated together. Finally, you must deal with people who don't want to go along with the movement or hold secret agendas and still find a way to build a broad consensus that welcomes a wide swath of stakeholders.

The key concept of leading like a movement is collective behavior. In essence, collective behavior is a moment in our society when people gather as a group to engage in some activity without being told to do so. Attending a scheduled weekly meeting is not collective behavior. Having a work conversation organically as you walk back to your desks from that meeting is collective behavior. As we've discussed before, leaving your comfortable silos to find partners at an intersection is a choice. You will likely never be told to do so. Therefore, when we look closely at leadership skills, we particularly consider those that are used when large groups come together for a single cause—that is, movements. What starts as one small group with a cause expands to a movement only when it begins to cut across many groups, united at an intersection of ideas.

In 1962, sociologist Neil Smelser studied the conditions necessary to induce people to gather as a crowd, which he collectively called value-added theory:[1]

1. **Structural conduciveness**: For a group to gather, participants must be generally aware of a problem and there must be a space available for them to gather in. (This is, one could argue, the result of a bunch of people who think like a system.)

2. **Structural strain**: Participants must also be aware that the problem is not being resolved, which causes them tension and frustration.

3. **Growth and spread of generalized belief**: People must then be able to agree on and name the problem and attribute it to something, which connects them together. (They, one could argue, act like a network.)

4. **Precipitating factors**: Some action or event then draws sudden, focused attention to the problem.

5. **Mobilization for action**: A leader or leaders emerge and start bringing direction and structure to the movement. (They lead like a movement.)

6. **Operation (failure) of social control**: Finally, authorities arrive and disperse the crowd, ostensibly to maintain order and the status quo.

A note on this final element of Smelser's theory, "operation (failure) of social control": The early 1960s was a transitional time in the United States, when social movements went from being commonly seen as the actions of unruly rabble-rousers to those of patriotic bravery. Smelser was a man of his times. We are not arguing that order is unimportant to a functioning society, but intersection work must rise above the status quo to succeed. It acknowledges that the way something has always been done is not a good enough reason to continue doing something that way. You don't have to take to the streets, but you do need to realize you can't do it all on your own. You won't so much be telling people what to do but rather bringing direction and establishing consensus on how to resolve the collectively agreed-upon problem.

 DETOUR: Leading like a movement through words

Interestingly, while Smelser was watching his theories in action at the University of California, Berkeley, where he taught, across the country the same theories could be connected to someone you wouldn't necessarily see as a leader acting outside traditional power structures. But then, John F. Kennedy was not your normal president of the United States.

To many, Kennedy won the election by challenging what he deemed a stagnant, reactionary foreign policy by the Eisenhower administration to the rise of the Cold War with Russia. His opponent, Richard Nixon, portrayed him as too young and inexperienced, but in a changing culture, that appeared to be exactly what made him popular.

Democracies offer a great structural cohesiveness for a social movement. Parties vying for power offer places for people to come together for rallies, and those people are generally united by a common awareness that there is a problem with the current person in the office and their candidate can fix it. The 1950s and early 1960s were a boiling pot for structural strain. The Korean War, the Hungarian Revolution, the Suez Crisis, and the

continued

construction of the Berlin Wall all pointed to a growing conflict between East and West.

A presidential race was the perfect place for growth and spread of generalized belief that the Republicans were too traditional and staid to handle this new world, and by the time Kennedy was elected, the Russians had the first satellite in space (Sputnik) and were readying Yuri Gagarin to become the first person to orbit Earth in April 1961.

A leader needed to emerge to bring about mobilization for action. Kennedy, in the summer of 1962, would emerge as that leader. He famously said, "We choose to go to the moon in this decade, not because that will be easy, but because it will be hard—because that goal will serve to organize and measure the best of our energies and skills—because that challenge is one we are willing to accept, one we are unwilling to postpone, and one we intend to win."[2]

But even for a leader with such authority, John F. Kennedy's speech didn't just come to light because he woke up one day and thought to himself, "It's about time we walked in space." Just over a year before that address, he told Congress that the United States "should commit itself to achieving the goal, before this decade is out, of landing a man on the Moon and returning him safely to the Earth."[3] A wonderful idea, certainly, but doing little to inspire belief in the probability of success. With Russia dominating the space race, the American people needed to be convinced that the tremendous use of resources and expense would lead to something that would capture their imaginations.

For every great speech, there is a great speechwriter. Behind the scenes, Ted Sorensen was accepting input from NASA and the Department of State, among other parties of interest, capturing the themes of exploration and using the space race to have peaceful competition with international rivals that were pertinent to both their brands. In fact, the line that would go down in history can be found in a nascent form in NASA's draft. Sorensen embellished it and Kennedy delivered it with passion. The delivery of this vision had become transformative by inviting other stakeholders to form a social movement that united them.

Let's return one last time to driving teacher Harold Smith. Once your car is in the flow of traffic, Smith explained, if you carve out enough space for yourself, you can create your own flow, because people naturally adjust to your speed as they too seek to find the flow. You are at once part of the crowd and also guiding it. People are responding to your choices, and by your actions, not by some declaration of control, they start seeing you as their leader. You set a powerful direction and inspire others to want to figure out how to make it work. This is leading like a movement.

In the following seven chapters, we'll take a deeper dive into each of the skills for *Lead Like a Movement*. As in the other sections, we'll devote a chapter to each skill:

- **Building diversity**
- **Integrating multiple logics**
- **Establishing feedback loops**
- **Saying no**
- **Managing dissonance**
- **Managing incumbents**
- **Managing secret agendas**

Let's start close to where we left off in our last section, *Act Like a Network*. You learned skills there like *Learning Other Professional Languages* and *Code-Mixing with Intention*. Using skills like those, you should have access to a diverse network. Here is your opportunity to take advantage of it as you begin to lead like a movement.

CHAPTER 23

Building Diversity

· ·

Social movements are often thought of as grassroots movements that use political skills to harness power for those marginalized in society. Social movements may use rallies, protests, social media, lobbying, marketing campaigns, or civil disobedience to produce results in society; they're credited with helping end slavery, end apartheid, expand voting rights, elect presidents (notably Barack Obama and Donald Trump in recent years), and many more powerful results.

Corporations and governments also use social movements to their advantage. Apple's 1997–2002 "Think Different" campaign showcased black-and-white photos of creative and revolutionary people, including Amelia Earhart, Thomas Edison, and Miles Davis, and movement leaders such as Mahatma Gandhi and Cesar Chavez. The work by art director Craig Tanimoto even featured that famous photo of flowers placed in gun barrels during the protest of the Vietnam War. This invitation for con-sumers to see Apple as not only a great product but also an opportunity to join a movement to think differently still resonates today. For instance, marketing consultant Katie Martell notes a similar phenomenon about the iPhone updates that have generated tremendous buzz in the 2010s and 2020s.

"Apple in particular tends to empower consumers with messaging about what they can do with their new iPhone," Martell says. She cites the 2020 campaign to share photos shot on the iPhone with the hashtag "#ShotoniPhone," which then were shared on those same billboards that 20 years earlier said, "Think Different." This tells these amateur photographers, "You've got that power in your hands." In a way, this is a social movement in its own right. It may not feel like classic social movements of protest and change, but that's part of the power—we get inspired and excited (if we resonate with the movement or campaign), and we don't even realize it is happening before we are part of something bigger than ourselves. "It's a different experience than you would feel with any other of their competitors," says Martell.[1]

Here's an important secret. All of these social movements, from corporate America, or from the left, right, or anywhere in between, work because of diversity. They harness different, often marginalized voices, bringing them together to create change and giving them access to power that has been denied them. In 2017, in the journal *Social Forces*, Ruud Wouters, a postdoctoral researcher at the University of Antwerp, released a study of recent demonstrations as diverse as for asylum in Europe and Black Lives Matter in the United States. Wouters noticed that demonstrations that mobilized more diverse participants, acting in unison, elicited broader support.

"A group of people that not only consists of the usual suspects but mirrors the diversity of the society on which behalf it claims to be speaking, simply has more democratic legitimacy," Wouters argues. "When people of all walks of life—conservatives and democrats, the young and the elderly, trade unions and environmental organizations—participate, a more credible claim of outside support can be made."[2] Martin Luther King Jr. knew this to be true for the civil rights movement. When he was jailed, he famously tried to recruit the very men who were holding the keys. He was "led to share with them that, after listening to their stories, they needed to join them in the marches, as they were as poor as us (earners wise) and that the only thing they had on their side was the false belief that because they were White, they were better."[3] When others can see that people can agree and come together, despite their differences, they are convinced they can join too. This grows the movement.

After you've brainstormed your role in the system and built the network, you'll need to lead and motivate people not only by connecting to who you need directly but also by encouraging them to build connections through the diversity in their own networks. You will be focused on bringing as many ships to sea as possible *and* creating opportunities for those ships to bring their own ships. There is a TED Talk we use in a lot of our presentations from Derek Sivers aptly titled "How to Start a Movement." In just three minutes, with a video playing in real time behind him, Sivers shows us how a movement takes off. At a music festival, we watch as one person dances alone. He's intense and a little bit foolish-looking.

"First, of course you know, a leader needs the guts to stand out and be ridiculed," Sivers tells us. "What he's doing is so easy to follow. Here's his first follower with a crucial role; he's going to show everyone else how to follow."[4] Because an intersection project brings people in across sectors, it increases the likelihood that they won't feel comfortable or familiar with your behaviors or actions as a leader, informed by your silo as they are. But "now it's not about the leader anymore," Sivers continues. "It's about them, plural. . . . The first follower is what transforms a lone nut into a leader." The follower calls to his friends, and before the three minutes is up—there is a mob of people dancing.

 Practicing building diversity

This sounds daunting. Nobody wants to be a "lone nut." But today, many tools exist to help you with determining and reaching the diversity of your network. The easiest tool, and one that you're likely familiar with, is LinkedIn. The main concept of the site, after all, is that you can expand your

continued

own personal network by having ready and easy access to your network's networks (and on and on, seemingly forever). Take advantage of the site's many robust search and research tools, such as searching for second and third connections. These more distantly connected individuals could be reached by those people on that network map who are the "boundary spanners" or "information brokers." Thanks to LinkedIn, you don't even have to ask for an introduction (though that's still a great strategy when available). You can just draw a direct network line yourself and send an invitation.

Some of these tools require a modest monthly charge, like the various premium features that can enhance your search criteria, but their functionality is well worth the added cost in our experience. Most people underutilize LinkedIn. You can learn almost anything important about someone in business, and you can deliver a message to their inbox at the click of a button. Once you have connected, you do the work of posting, but then your posts do the work for you to gather and expand the force through the likes and reposts that amplify its message. It will also gain you new connections. That's why social networks can be such quick amplifiers to allow people and their ideas to go "viral." Reddit and TikTok have both been huge forums in recent years to build movements that unite people from all walks of life.

At the intersection, where you are likely working with a more formal institution, Facebook Ads and Google Ads also allow for robust targeting of possible connections. While not inexpensive, Facebook Ads allow for deep micro-targeting of backgrounds and professional and personal interests. Facebook Groups have emerged as a powerful, and free, way of finding people with specific interests. With over ten million Facebook groups and over 1.8 billion active monthly users, these groups allow you to find people with just about any passion or interest you can imagine.[5] Don't forget to utilize more traditional network-building organizations like your high school or college alumni office, which can be invaluable for locating people in specific industries or people with specific skills. Many alumni offices or college career offices have robust search capabilities that they'll share with fellow graduates of the institution.

Finally, we've found targeting specific topic areas with Google Alerts to be particularly fruitful. You can receive daily alerts related to your areas of interest. Using specific search terms in Google Alerts, you can learn who is doing very specific work. For example, Cleve has an alert set for "Social Entrepreneurship," and he receives a weekly (or daily, depending on how he sets his preferences) summary of news, people, and events from around the world on this topic of great interest to him. Many times, he has reached out to people or organizations he has learned about through these alerts, and they have become collaborators on projects. Try setting alerts for any topic that interests you or for which you may want to find collaborators. You'll immediately find some of the most active people and organizations doing work in that area. This will allow you to build the diversity of individuals, issues, goals, and tactics you bring to your field of interest. Combining these search results with a detailed dive into LinkedIn, you can begin building a robust, powerfully diverse network with ease.

However, diversity is not enough on its own. You may invite different boats into the water, but if they don't feel welcome or comfortable, it won't be long until they raise the sails and seek safer waters. This is one of the biggest reasons movements eventually lose their muster, whether they be the ones on the streets where the unity wanes and people go home, or in the office buildings, where new voices get tired of not feeling listened to and not having a true seat at the table, so they move on or are ousted. If you want the diverse voices you invite in to then invite in more diverse voices, the environment must be generative and inclusive. The next few skills on our list accomplish just that.

CHAPTER 24

Integrating Multiple Logics

. . . .

To lead movements, you need to actively understand and work with what's going on under the hood of your partnership. This is where the concept of institutional logic is helpful. An institutional logic is a set of practices and beliefs that influence how an institution operates, makes decisions, and helps individuals in the organization understand what constitutes success. For example, in an engineering firm, a prevailing institutional logic may be precision, while in a social service organization, it could be compassion. Yet institutions operate with multiple, simultaneous logics, and they can be contradictory. For example, the social service organization needs to gain funding to operate as a business, thus its compassion logic is mixed with market or financial logics. The engineering firm may need to reduce costs to defeat the competition in addition to its more dominant logic of precision. America relies on the institutional logics of democracy and capitalism—the people's will does not always have the same needs as a free market.

This is deeper than, although certainly related to, culture. Biologist Brian Skerry says, "Behavior is what we do. Culture is how we do it."[1] Institutional logic, perhaps, is *why* we do it. Take successful corporations, argues Harvard professor Rosabeth Moss Kanter. "In those firms, society and people are not afterthoughts or inputs to be used and discarded but are core to their purpose," she notes. While certainly all firms need to make money, "in their choices of how to do so, [great companies] think about building enduring institutions. They invest in the future while being aware of the need to build people and society."[2] It is no surprise, Kanter points out, that these organizations work at the intersections effectively. They build partnerships, from Proctor & Gamble co-creating worldwide safe water and hospital programs to IBM providing software to track relief supplies and reunite families with aid organizations after natural disasters. These, in turn, build their brand, rebuild areas in which their employees need to work and live, and support economic growth of new consumer markets. The logic is both to do good and to build an efficient and profitable business.

Like culture, however, an institution's true logics are quite often invisible; even the people who work within that logic are not consciously aware of it. Your ability to recognize and work with these logics is essential because doing so allows you to have insight into managing the many logics working within the initiative. Each partner or person brings their own institutional logic with them, and their logics can be conflicting. The ability to manage multiple logics is critical to the project's success. This can be tough! To oversimplify it a bit, business leaders are still ultimately looking for profit, government leaders are often looking for impact within a highly regimented and rule-bound culture, and nonprofit leaders are often trying to make a difference with enormous financial constraints. In reality, hundreds or more logics operate simultaneously, and each initiative has a unique combination of logics.

The people with whom you are collaborating are embedded in their own systems that may have very different logics from each other. What may seem like a small thing to you might completely rock their boat. So before you can manage all these logics, you must first identify them. How can you do that? Many nonprofits don't talk about their value propositions or the ratio of their costs to expenses for their products even if these things *do* matter, but for corporations this is the quite literal "bottom line" and will likely be front and center.

Practicing integrating multiple logics

THE BUSINESS MODEL CANVAS

Key Partners	Key Activities	Value Propositions	Customer Relationships	Customer Segments
People or organizations you have purposely added to your network to enhance your impact	The actions you take that allow your service or product to be successful	Looking to the left or right, what makes you competitive or attractive	The ways the people or companies who buy or use your product or output feel valued	The people or companies who you have found that are drawn to or consume your product or output—ideally you group these people or companies so that you can focus your efforts at reaching them.
	Key Resources The resources or people you already have that make you uniquely qualified to do this work		**Channels** How you reach the people or companies that buy or use your product or output	

Cost Structure	Revenue Streams
How you break down your expenses to finance your partners, activities, and resources	How you break down what your customers are willing to pay through their relationships, segments, and channels

To try to understand your partners' logics, repurpose the popular (and publicly sourced) Business Model Canvas (BMC).[3] A BMC is a one-page assignment that asks you to list the key partners, activities, and resources and the cost structure they contribute to the business on one side of the page, and customer relationships, segments, and channels and the revenue streams they contribute to on the other side, with the value propositions that tie them together in the middle. You typically either begin or end with value propositions, discovering or building from the value that you offer that makes you attractive and competitive. Understanding value propositions is an imperfect, but useful, stand-in for individual institutional logics. Sketch out a very basic, general-level BMC for each of your partners to think about their business from their view. Estimating how the things that contribute to their costs create value for the things that create their revenue provides a window into the intentions behind their operations, highlighting the relationships between the inputs and outputs. In business, you learn that you need a single value proposition so that your customers understand why your product will improve their lives. However, when you look at

continued

businesses or business decisions with outside eyes, you will inevitably find multiple value propositions. Multiple logics for what the organization is trying to accomplish have somehow, for those on the inside, become singular.

For example, a hospital operates according to many conflicting logics. There's the logic of the limitless value proposition of healing and health, while simultaneously there's the logic of efficiency. The successful hospital leader balances these competing logics (and many others) and crafts them into a single logic that maintains the focus on health and healing within the enormous constraints of efficiency and limited resources. You may know this instinctively, but looking at the revenue streams (health and healing) and costs (efficiency and limited resources) can truly bring this value proposition to light.

LOGIC MODEL TEMPLATE

Problem Statement
A succinct summary of the core problem your company, program, or organization is trying to solve through your work

Goals
Specific and measurable goals you're trying to achieve toward solving the problem with your work

Outcomes
Changes in behavior, milestones, and infrastructure occurring as a result of the activities and outputs you've generated

Rationales	Resources	Activities	Outputs
Beliefs about how change occurs based on the work you're undertaking (I.e., this connects and shows how your goals will be served by the resources and activities you're providing.)	What expertise you, your organization, and partners can bring to create activities that will help reach the goals you've outlined	Quantifiable number of participants, revenue, and easily measurable indicators of the results of your efforts	The activities in which your customers or participants will engage through your venture

External Factors
Economic climate, partnership dynamics, and any factors outside of your control that will affect your success

Another tool, often used by those in the nonprofit and philanthropic sectors, is called the logic model. The logic model is a tool in which the organization or partnership states the problem that they're trying to solve and then articulates how their resources, activities, outputs, and outcomes work to solve the problem.[4] For nonprofits in particular, this might be a more worthy exercise than a BMC to uncover logics. It literally has the word "logic" in it!

You can create a BMC or a logic model for your partners or potential partners, or a partnership you're hoping to create. We've found this to be an enormously helpful exercise, as it helps to surface the logics, assumptions, and approaches that are often hidden in partnerships and often get in the way later. Once you know the underlying logics, and where multiple logics exist, you can work with them and create the levers for impact that can result when multiple logics work together as part of a well-coordinated whole.

CHAPTER 25

Establishing Feedback Loops

. . . .

In a study of over 50,000 executives, leadership consultants Jack Zenger and Joseph Folkman found a very clear message. Leaders who ranked at the top 10 percent in asking for feedback were also near the top in their overall leadership effectiveness.[1] You must regularly seek feedback from and give feedback to your potential partners. A host of studies shows direct correlation of feedback to performance. We succeed when we truly know how our performance is doing and what we can do to fix it. Having this foundation of self-awareness engenders trust. And trust is the foundation of leadership.

Back to our driving analogy—getting through an intersection safely isn't just a matter of how safely you proceed alone. It's also a matter of communicating intentions with other intersection users, locking eyes with the other driver at the stop sign or with the pedestrian attempting to cross in front of you. Someone needs to make a gesture of their intentions, and the other person needs to respond with feedback to that gesture. It is essential to create a space in the complexity of intersections that balances multiple perspectives from all our silos/cars so that people can simultaneously embrace their worldview and recognize that their worldview is just one side of the story.

One of our most successful feedback practices at our firm is "strong opinions, loosely held." With our clients, we give ourselves a lot of latitude to have strong opinions, delivered tactfully and respectfully, of course. But we also hold these opinions loosely. That means we're open to changing our opinions based on what we learn from what our clients are thinking. And because the opinions are loosely held, we don't try to persuade the other person. It doesn't become a power struggle. We're learning from one another and hearing one another, and it's OK that we may disagree.

 ## Practicing establishing feedback loops

Our proudest moments are when we start hearing our clients say, "Strong opinion, loosely held" before weighing in during a conversation among themselves that we are facilitating. We often borrow from the world of improvisation to encourage this practice. In improv, actors are required to perform a scene without a script, making it up as they go along. The only way they can do this is to take what one person says and add to it. They use a technique called "yes, and." "This house we are standing in sure is huge." "Yes, and our aunt must have been very rich." "Yes, and I'm so excited we inherited it." Together, they co-create an idea.

If one person said, "The house we are standing in sure is huge" and the other person said, "No, it's small," there really isn't anywhere to go with that idea. In a brainstorm, if you say something like, "That's interesting; that makes me think of this other thing," that's, in effect, "yes and-ing" that idea. You are more likely to show your best ideas if they don't get immediately shot down, but you also can't let your pride get in the way. It's everyone's responsibility to share their strong opinion too and build toward the best, fullest idea.

Another related and equally powerful feedback process we use extensively is the "Door Opening Draft." (Daniel often calls this the "Messy First Draft" . . . which may be saying something about how he writes?) For anything to be created, someone has to step out first. It's a risk to put the first ideas out for exploration and development (first penguin to the rescue!), and it requires a willingness to expose yourself to the feedback. Partners working together at an intersection can talk about how to do something to death, but somebody has to volunteer to act, even if it's messy. It is always easier to edit and refine anything than it is to start it. Naming things gives them power; calling this first action "messy" or "door opening" helps the person feel safe in creating it and others feel safe in building on it with their own visions and opinions. From there, you can offer strong opinions, loosely held, that "yes, and" the ideas to give them more clarity and strength, and the power of the collective voice of your intersection. A great way to do this is through a combination of suggested edits on a program like MS Word or Google Docs and comments in the margin that are framed as questions. These work because they don't assume superiority or finality of idea—they don't just change the text to what the editor thinks is right—but in a culture in which it is expected that people are simply trying to build off the initial idea, give feedback, and strengthen the idea, they are nevertheless usually accepted.

Finally, while many often speak about how to give feedback, they don't always talk about the timing of the feedback. In theater, there is a big difference between a vague piece of feedback the director gives an actor in the first week of rehearsal when they are just exploring, a direct piece of feedback the director gives them in the middle when they are finding details and making choices about their movement and actions, and an enabling and manageable piece of feedback you give them the night before the show. You wouldn't tell them right before they step onstage that they should consider delivering their lines in a completely different accent. "OK, now go have fun out there!"

In other words, despite popular belief, the aim of feedback is actually not to ensure that the right idea wins. The aim is to enable the best result. The night before a plan is due to be presented at a big meeting is not when someone needs to think deeply about the structure or content. They need something that will allow them to deliver the content, for better or for worse, as strongly and clearly as possible. Intersections, crossing sectors and silos, and the diversity of people and cultures included bring a wide array of feedback needs. You may need to self-censor your feedback in moments of instability even if you are right. Remember, Americans need a good pat on the back mixed in or we go crazy with despair!

The point to all of this is that as leaders at the intersection, we need to get good at giving and receiving feedback and, perhaps more importantly, at developing systems within which others feel welcome to give us feedback. Because, let's be honest, often we don't really want feedback; we want validation. But validation isn't helpful because it keeps us where we are. We need to know what people are really thinking—and quickly so that we can course-correct and help get our work back on target. This can become more complicated if we're concerned that giving or receiving honest feedback will disappoint others. We want them to like us. To combat this, we have set up systems for everyone to feel heard and included.

CHAPTER 26

Sharing the Economy without Leaving the House

. . . .

Sitting in the Airbnb headquarters, Chip Conley, Airbnb's head of hospi-tality, discussed the quote often attributed to Gandhi, "First they ignore you, then they ridicule you, then they fight you, and then you win." Conley's invoking of Gandhi makes it clear how much the titans of the sharing economy like Airbnb, Lyft, and others see their work as an inter-twining of social movement and business. They're harnessing something deeper in us—to not only participate in the economy but also shape it and use its power to transform society. Perhaps this is part of the secret to how the largest hotelier in the world owns no hotel rooms and the largest taxi company owns no cars. These companies are mobilizing us to transform our relationships with our most prized and expensive personal possessions—and share them.

Our grandparents never would have believed that we'd be renting rooms in our own home to complete strangers. Even more inconceivable, they'd be amazed that we'd spend the day traversing the freeways and city streets responding to electronic ride solicitations in the very same car we used to drive the kids to school in the morning. That's part of the mystique and brilliance of the sharing economy. It takes commonplace activities that we do every day and may take for granted and, with the power of technology, develops new ways to earn a profit, interact, and shift cultures.

While for many, the choice to drive for a ride-sharing service or host Airbnb guests is undeniably economic, that's often not the predominant way Airbnb leads. They focus on movement leadership. They're not just perceived as a hotel chain—they're also seen as part of a cultural experience. Without an actual product, they couldn't simply make top-down decisions on how people would use their services to travel. Instead, they helped people re-envision what travel could mean and pointed them in a direction to work together to revolutionize the industry.

Building diversity

Airbnb celebrates diversity, authentically; it helps build their brand and their business. One look at their website and their offerings and you can see a diversity of accommodations from mansions to caves and from tents to condos. They've even created their own version of concierge services through their Airbnb Experiences—classes and tours across the world. You can find cooking classes offered remotely from a small village home in Mumbai, take a virtual tour of Prague with a plague doctor, or learn to make Italian pasta with grandmas from their kitchens in Florence. The opportunities are endless, celebrating uniqueness and diversity rather than the uniformity that has become the norm of so much of the hospitality business. Because so much diversity of expression and background is welcomed in Airbnb, many new people become part of the movement that is supporting Airbnb. For those on Airbnb, the company, in addition to providing an economic livelihood, is allowing people to pursue their passions, their art, and their contributions to society. This is inspiring to many and likely brings a lot more allegiance and growth to the company than if they were simply trying to motivate people financially.

Integrating multiple logics

Given how common Airbnb has become, it is easy to lose sight of the fact that it started with a millennial wanting to earn money by renting an air mattress on his floor (the company was originally called Airbed and Breakfast). Now the company offers accommodations in over 34,000 cities and 191 countries and often transcends vast political and cultural divides insurmountable for traditional hotel brands.[1] They're managing a brand that is simultaneously offering accommodations in the West Bank, Korea, and remote Peru. The cultural gaps they're overcoming are almost indescribable.

In our section on leading like a movement, we discussed the skill of utilizing multiple logics as essential to moving forward when working at the intersection of sectors. Airbnb is a perfect example of this. Of course, Airbnb embraces the logic of hospitality and adventure. That's what you'd expect a hospitality company to do.

More subtly on display here, in an industry known for creating uniformity and perfectionism, they've built a culture that celebrates the individuality, even quirkiness, of each accommodation and the uniqueness of the individual hosts. Further, Airbnb has incorporated the logics of service and giving. They make us feel like we're giving back to a culture (or a family) by staying with one of their hosts. People go out of their way to express a personal touch to welcome their guests, and it is reflected to them through small gestures in showing care toward their property that one never would give when staying in a hotel. Embracing this logic of service and giving has also served Airbnb well when regulations are proposed against them. Public meetings are often filled with hosts who speak out in favor of Airbnb because of the financial and cultural contributions to communities.

Buried just below the surface here is a logic common to many movements—the human need for connection. Airbnb recognizes something that can be found across corporate, nonprofit, and governmental business sectors. All business is personal. Movements tie people together. They bond over a shared cause or a shared experience. The so-called sharing economy is supposed to make us feel connected personally to one another. But the truth is often far from this imagined reality. Ride sharing has slowly felt more and more like a taxi service, but Airbnb has, by and large, built its core business and its business expansions while keeping the personal connection front and center.

It is not a surprise that their slogan is "belong anywhere." Airbnb has built its entire business model on an invitation for others to join their movement.

Establishing feedback loops

Like many sharing-economy companies, Airbnb has built two-way feedback systems where both the consumer and the provider of the service are rated and give each other feedback. This is becoming so commonplace that we barely notice it, but imagine if a traditional hotel chain rated its guests and gave them feedback on how they cared for the room and interacted with front desk staff. The effects of these feedback loops are many. Of course, the ratings help future users gauge the quality of the accommodations. More subtly, the ratings serve to build the movement and give feedback to it. When a user or host takes steps "pleasing" to the other, they get rewarded with higher ratings. When one or the other goes against the norms of what is expected, they get penalized with a lower rating. This feedback helps guide and shape the movement, ultimately giving it a lot more responsiveness than the ubiquitous surveys that so many companies request of their consumers. A survey also does little to shape the behavior of the consumer—another reason the two-way feedback system is so powerful. It makes the consumer feel responsible for the movement in subtle ways.[2]

This is a real-life version of our "yes, and" improvisation. A user or host gives feedback that causes the other to want to improve something, and that improvement is then visible to their next user or host. They can respond to the suggestion with what they think they can do about it and see what happens. The next user or host can respond to this improvement with yet another suggestion, and the collective back-and-forth builds better experiences for all. Airbnb recognizes that solutions to good service are best when crowd-sourced—hosts learn to host, and consumers learn to consume through openly exchanging feedback with one another, and everyone wins as a result.

Managing dissonance, incumbents, and secret agendas

As we move into the second half of our *Lead Like a Movement* section, you will see ways in which people leading like a movement are able to build a coalition that helps inspire a vision while simultaneously managing dissonance, incumbents, and secret agendas.

Jeff Jordan from the famed venture capital firm Andreessen Horowitz—Facebook, Twitter, and Skype, to name a few successful investments—said that "the first time I heard about Airbnb I thought it was possibly the stupidest idea I've ever heard." As founder Brian Chesky said it, "People thought we were crazy. They said strangers never stay with strangers and horrible things are going to happen."[3]

But when Jordan met Chesky for his pitch, things changed quickly. "I went from complete skeptic to complete believer in twenty-nine minutes," Jordan said. "Every great founder can really tell a great story. It's one of the key things in a founder, that you can convince people to believe."

Airbnb faces obstacles from many directions—competitors like large hotel chains, regulations from hundreds of thousands of governmental bodies across the globe in diverse cultures and languages, and, of course, scrutiny from the media for unfortunate actions perpetrated by a small number of guests or hosts.

Airbnb has overcome these obstacles by managing dissonance, incumbents, and secret agendas in large and small ways. To build an early coalition of support, they managed early dissatisfaction with the service by visiting all of their hosts in their launch city, New York, and staying with them, writing detailed reviews and using their design backgrounds to set up and photograph the space.[4]

Now a giant corporation, Airbnb utilizes many tools to build its coalition—one of the most potent of these, especially when it was going through a massive growth phase, was Airbnb Open, an in-person gathering of over 7,000 hosts and key partners from over 100 countries. The massive, eclectic event helped people see that the company was much more than a technology firm. Masterminded by Conley—and highlighting his knack for fun, powerful events and building a team—the event was able to showcase the expectations, aspirations, and opportunities for Airbnb's brand and partners. The timing of these events was crucial because the company was simultaneously facing lawsuits and protests over what some saw as discriminatory practices. The event provided a powerful counter narrative to its most important supporters—its hosts—in a way that no corporate communication could ever have accomplished.

Airbnb continues building its coalitions not only with its hosts but also with corporate accounts (of which it has over 35,000) and even with big hotel brands that have come to realize that Airbnb can be a strategic partner. It has started collecting hotel taxes to support the economies of the cities it services and has pledged to give data to help those governments improve their tourism industries.[5] The coalition skills they've utilized have been essential to their success. We will dive into this and related skills in the second half of this section.

The path forward

Like all movements, Airbnb continues to change and evolve and face crisis points. For the company, leading like a movement will likely serve them into the future. They don't have a choice at this point. Indeed, they've recently taken steps to double down on their movement leadership by starting Airbnb.org, a nonprofit that connects "people to places to stay in times of crisis."[6] With this organization, Airbnb has formed partnerships with the Red Cross, Mercy Corps, and other relief organizations. Furthermore, with the COVID-19 pandemic and outbreak of war in Ukraine, donating to Airbnb.org to provide stays for essential workers and refugees became a powerful way for individuals across the world to contribute to social causes. This new organization and its focus show that partnerships and movement leadership are only becoming more important to Airbnb's work into the future.

Despite all it has done to build diversity, integrate multiple logics, and establish feedback loops, Airbnb continues its success in large part because it knows what it is and, perhaps more importantly, what it is not. It helps people travel and connect to the people who live in the places they are traveling to. Likewise, sometimes we best serve an intersection collaboration by saying no to opportunities and ideas that don't serve the larger goals of our work.

CHAPTER 27

Saying No

. . . .

It may strike you as ironic that after spending much of the book asking you to observe, empathize with, and embody the perspectives of others, we now offer you a whole chapter on the word "no." Saying no, however, is the ultimate expression of strategy and is essential for leading like a movement. It demonstrates focus, directness, and relevance. Harvard Business School's Michael Porter reminds us that "Strategy 101 is about choices: You can't be all things to all people. The essence of strategy is that you must set limits on what you're trying to accomplish."[1]

Many of the best companies, organizations, and agencies are focused. Michelin star restaurants sell only high-end ingredients that are cooked to perfection and presented with artistry. McDonald's wants you to get your food quickly. They each appeal to specific clientele as a result. When we are at intersections, the temptation is to do quick food that is also high-end artistry. Each partner brings their own style, and the easiest thing is to try to either let all of them coexist or squish them into one compromised box that serves none of them. We're all trying to do everything, all at once, and together we're successful at way too little. We get burned out, our stakeholders and clients don't know our strengths, and our offerings suffer.

One of the best ways to remain focused is to learn when to say no.

You've got to be crystal clear on your strengths and those areas where your organization's or partnership's purpose or mission are best served.

Software developers sometimes speak of trying to eliminate "cruft," or poorly designed, unnecessary, or outdated features that take up memory and slow down the software's user functionality. Cruft is annoying and slows everything down, making the experience unpleasant. The insidious thing about cruft is that most of us don't see it; it operates in the background, invisible to most users while sucking away our time, energy, and productivity.

Cruft operates in our organizations and partnerships as well. In this case, it manifests in many forms, especially in old procedures, initiatives, and programs that once seemed like a good idea but actually slow down the work. This cruft may be better done by another team, organization, or partnership or may need to be completely eliminated. Be on the lookout for this in your own team or organization and in your partnerships, and say no. Says Satoru Iwata, the much-loved president and CEO of Nintendo, "When you figure out exactly 'What is necessary for this game,' a world of possibilities will open up. So rather than tossing in whatever you want, it's good to remember the creative power of paring back."[2]

 Practicing saying no

You can learn what to say no to by gaining clarity on your personal strengths and purpose with a simple activity. Start by listing the top 10–15 activities you spend your professional time on. These could be mundane activities, like checking email, balancing accounts, or running team meetings. They could also be more specific tasks, like designing programs, drafting building plans, or conducting audits. The key is to be honest with yourself and include everything, even the most mundane of tasks, that you most often do.

Next, plot your activities on a two-by-two grid. Use the horizontal axis for your competency or skill in completing the activity, and use the vertical axis for the contribution of the activity to your mission or your organization's mission. If we're being honest with ourselves, most of us have activities in all four quadrants. Those activities in the bottom quadrants (weak skills and low importance to the mission on the left, strong skills and low importance to the mission on the right) are strong candidates for elimination because they have little to do with your or your organization's mission. Activities in the bottom-left quadrant are particularly wasteful because you're not good at them and they don't have relevance to your mission. Activities in the bottom-right quadrant feel good to accomplish because you're good at them, but they don't have anything to do with your mission. For us, email management is a good example of a bottom-right-quadrant activity: we are both good at it and it feels good to have a well-managed email inbox, but neither our nor our organization's mission is to process email.

The four quadrants could look like this:

1. We could be unskilled at construction, and it's not important to intersection work (bottom left).

2. Tax law is important to intersection work, but we aren't skilled at it (top left).

3. We could be skilled at gardening, but it's not important to intersection work. Or even we could be skilled at leading teams, but it's not AS important to intersection work (bottom right).

4. We could be skilled at leading across partnerships, and that IS important to intersection work (top right).

continued

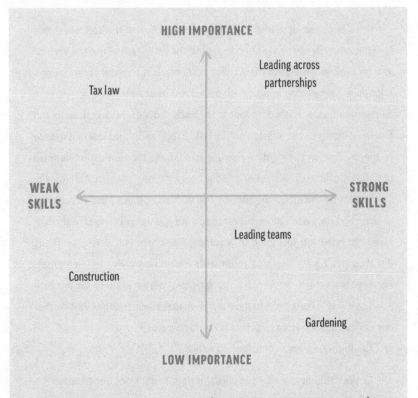

Activities in the top-left quadrant (weak skills and high importance) are likely best outsourced because someone else can do them better than you can, and they need to be done. Indeed, most of your time and energy should be spent in those activities in the top-right quadrant, where your skills are strong and the value to the mission is high. Activities in all the other quadrants are good candidates for saying no.

You can bring this same two-by-two exercise to the intersection once you've recognized the multitude of perspectives that people are bringing from behind each of the wheels of their cars (or boats).[3] It forces you to bring the multiple logics you've identified, for the first time, into a single statement of what you are all doing and what you should be doing. Instead of an organization's mission, you are looking at the mission of the intersection. You can surface disagreements by seeing who put what as low mission relevance when others put similar things as high mission relevance. Someone will have to say no to something for the sake of the partnership, even if it operates within their own team's, organization's, or sector's logic. Instead of your organization's competencies, you are looking at the intersection's competencies. There hopefully should be more of these because there are partners who can fill in each other's gaps. You can see what elements can be done together and what needs to potentially be split off to capture individual or sector strengths.

You'll face seemingly endless demands on your time, and we encourage you to harness that creative power of doing fewer, more focused activities to achieve your goals. Why go through all the complications of intersection work if, in the end, you can't decipher who and what you should put your energy into? It's a lot easier if everyone at the intersection has been as purposeful as you in their choice to be there. We hope you have learned enough about systems to position yourself to observe if that is truly the reality. But ultimately, all you can know and all you can actually control is if it serves *your* needs. If it doesn't, simply drive on.

If it does, this is where the work begins. Because to implement a shared vision, you need real, across-the-board buy-in. You now need to not just make decisions but implement them too. And this is best done not by compromise but by consensus. A general agreement on a shared view of what is best for everyone.

But no matter what you do, not *everyone* is going to agree. With that in mind, we're going to move on to the last three skills, which are about some of the common and often difficult and painful challenges to overcome in leading like a movement: *Managing Dissonance, Managing Incumbents,* and *Managing Secret Agendas.* At some point, your work as a leader will be done, and you will have to move on, but what you've created needs to sustain. The unique challenge of intersection work is that you don't have the power you typically have at an independent organization to control the product after its release. Other partners may be managing it, or it will splinter off and become an organization unto itself. At that point, you are no longer the leader; the coalition is. And you need to build that coalition strong.

CHAPTER 28

Managing Dissonance

. . . .

At this point, you've decided what you're not going to do, and you've reached consensus around how to move the project forward. This is where the unity built around the exploration and growth of an idea gets to shine. An infrastructure needs to survive past its birth, and to do so, it must have built-in systems that give it the strength to withstand challenges and a dynamic culture that will welcome even more folks and keep the momentum building.

Remember that negotiation we all do at a four-way stop sign intersection, locking eyes and providing some recognition to each other of who's turn it is to go? Preferably, that gesture is one of offering for another to take a turn and the response is a wave of gratitude. As we all know, however, this isn't always the way it plays out. Sometimes you need to address less productive behaviors. And typically, by this point, your intersection is not a four-way stop sign. It's an intersection where all the traffic lights are out. The honeymoon is over, and lots of challenges are popping up everywhere. This is the hard work to protect the unity you've created.

To do so, you must find a way to incorporate and value dissonant voices, even if you find what they are saying and how they are saying it completely counterproductive. No matter what direction an initiative is heading, there will always be struggles and challenges. Some people will have competing visions for the work. They'll want to move in one way, while the group is moving in another. This dissonance can be productive and helpful, or it can become destructive if not managed well.

Years ago, Dr. Stephen Karpman introduced the concept of the drama triangle. According to his concept, when people are under stress, they take on three dysfunctional roles—the victim (damsel in distress), the persecutor (villain), and the rescuer (hero).[1] All too often, when there is dissent in group dynamics, we perceive villainy. You might find yourself reaching across your intersection to a partner for agreement on an idea, but you see that partner is prevented from agreeing with you, or so you think, by a third person who disagrees with your idea. That partner then becomes a damsel in distress, being held against their will by the third person (the villain).

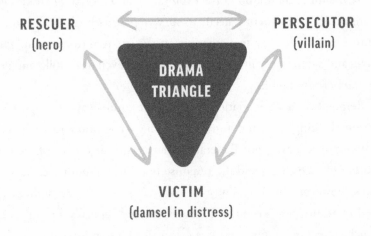

RESCUER (hero) — PERSECUTOR (villain)

DRAMA TRIANGLE

VICTIM (damsel in distress)

As a person now quite adept at intersection skills, you will likely find yourself positioned to play the hero, stepping in for that partner whose vision you have so painfully nurtured and unified with your own. This aids them in nothing except shirking responsibility for their participation in the dissonance, which probably only came to be because the person who seems like the villain feels outnumbered and worried they will soon become the victim themselves. Of course, in real life, often a victim is truly in a powerless situation. However, in the context of the drama triangle, there is a built-in assumption that the person who feels like a victim is building a false narrative that says they have no control over their circumstances. To protect themselves, they shrink inward and stop communicating their needs, playing a role in a vicious cycle that only ends up hurting them more.

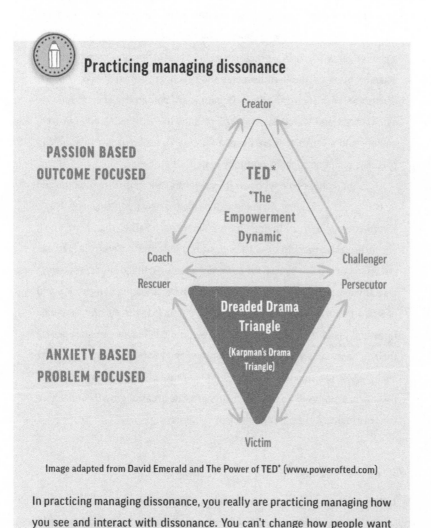

Practicing managing dissonance

Creator

PASSION BASED
OUTCOME FOCUSED

TED*
*The Empowerment Dynamic

Coach

Challenger

Rescuer

Persecutor

Dreaded Drama Triangle
(Karpman's Drama Triangle)

ANXIETY BASED
PROBLEM FOCUSED

Victim

Image adapted from David Emerald and The Power of TED* (www.powerofted.com)

In practicing managing dissonance, you really are practicing managing how you see and interact with dissonance. You can't change how people want

continued

to behave or act. You can only empower them to have an option to behave and act differently.

David Emerald shows us that we can turn the drama triangle into The Empowerment Dynamic (TED*). His TED* shifts the victim from the bottom of the triangle to the top and reorients them as a creator. A creator doesn't feel powerless; in fact, they show a resiliency to make empowered choices. They have exposed their silo to a powerful new way of thinking and have willingly put themselves at risk to do so. The persecutor becomes a challenger who trusts a process that enables them and others to be held accountable. And the hero becomes the coach, encouraging clarity in the discussion with their questions. Debate is framed as healthy, dissonance as expected and welcomed. Instead of allowing actions to emerge from anxiety and a sense of there being an unfixable problem, the relationship becomes about actionable, mutually beneficial outcomes.

It is unlikely people who see themselves as victims or feel victimized by being cast as villains are going to flip this triangle by themselves. That's where you come in. By taking on the role of coach rather than hero, you'll encourage the others to view their positions differently. Your role is to ask questions to ensure clarity from the disagreeing collaborators. You won't attach yourself to one side or the other, instead showing compassion and positive reinforcement for any surfacing conflict. If the coach uses questions and insights to allow others to grow, the challenger can start seeing their honesty as a way for others to grow, and soon the creator can start seeing their position as resiliency, an inspirational gift of growth as well. Dissonance allows all to see the challenges, the areas of growth, and where the true moments of productivity can be found.

Let's look at a real-life example from a professional coach. We come to this story via Stephen Dubner, the cohost of the podcast *No Stupid Questions*.[2] Dubner quotes longtime coach of the Pittsburgh Steelers Mike

Tomlin after the Steelers had beaten the rival team Baltimore Ravens (Daniel's Baltimore friends of his youth would hate him for using this example, but oh well). Tomlin had said, "I thought [the game] was far from perfect, but I thought collectively our guys did not blink. No one sought comfort." Seeking comfort, Tomlin explained, was doing those "things that people do under duress, that when given the opportunity to look back at it, they wish they hadn't, to lessen their roles when things get tough. That's one of the things we openly talk about. Don't minimize your role when things are tough, have ownership over what's transpiring. Don't blame others, don't state problems. Let's openly talk about solutions as opposed to stating the obvious."

The skill to manage dissonance in a healthy way is to share your passion for doing the work and accomplishing the goals and to set clear outcomes to strive toward. You don't need to be a hero, swooping in and saving the day by solving the problems for your coalition. You need to teach them to solve the problems themselves; you need to be the coach. You do need to be completely in control, but not of the product, just the process. This gives you the strong ground to stand on as you encourage self-responsibility. Set expectations on how much time will be given to engage disagreement, and create one-on-one opportunities to listen and support but not advise. The TED* and other frameworks like it simply become a way to explain in a common language the values you have already made clear in your actions.

Dissonance is all around you and will come up as a natural part of working at the intersection. You need to be ever vigilant for it and ready with tools to manage it and move forward productively. This brings us to the related topic of managing incumbents, who are frequently the primary source of a lot of the dissonance found at the intersection.

CHAPTER 29

Managing Incumbents

. . . .

Managing incumbents refers to the challenges of managing the people and organizations already in place. Current systems often reinforce the status quo, and they have a lot of momentum to keep doing what they're already doing the way they've been doing it for a very long time. Innovators and intersection leaders often disrupt that status quo, however. People working in the existing system will push to keep that system running as it is and, consciously or unconsciously, will try to undermine or discredit new entrants. At an intersection, every system needs to shift to build a new one collaboratively on top of them. This will only multiply the resistance. You. Will. Want. To. Pull. Your. Hair. Out.

This discrediting comes in a variety of forms. The most common way that incumbents discredit new people or processes is by challenging their effectiveness. There is power in not getting discouraged by the disagreement of those who "had their chance" to make something new. There is not, however, an easy path to building trust with incumbents.

It is critical to be constantly in touch with and aware of the moves and approaches of incumbents. They have a lot to lose, and your entry into their space is likely quite threatening to them. Depending on your initiative, the incumbents may be undermining your work and reputation in small ways, such as not attending meetings or sending opinionated emails to express their frustration. Or their efforts might be much bigger, such as paying high-priced lobbyists to create regulations or other barriers to your success. The old adage, "Keep your friends close and your enemies closer," is as true as ever in working with incumbents. Except, of course, they are not your enemies, though they may feel like they are. They are threatened by your presence. You'll want to regularly engage with them, understand them, and learn from them and about them. And keep them engaged and speaking with you so you can be aware of their moves.

One possible reframe you can make for yourself, just as the TED* triangle renamed the villain as a challenger, is to rename incumbents as historians. They have seen others try to build unified visions and watched those intersections collapse under mismanagement and unstable alliances. Or perhaps by doing the work you're doing, you're threatening their business, funding, or livelihood. Their personal experience has taught them that the change you seek will simply lead to endless complications and make their lives worse, not better. They've seen this story before. They are the historians, and they understand nuances that you may not be able to see.

So, to show incumbents you value history and their place as holders of it, start by thinking like a historian.

 ### Practicing managing incumbents

In the *Harvard Business Review* article "Your Company's History as a Leadership Tool," John T. Seaman Jr. and George David Smith detailed a story about the 2010 acquisition of the historic British brand Cadbury by the oh-so-American Kraft Foods.[1] To ward off potential cultural conflict, using their archives, Kraft launched an intranet site titled "Coming Together," which showcased the unlikely historical alignment of the organizations. It turned out both had been driven by the devout faith of their founders to give back to their communities, for instance. The site also featured, we are happy to report, a road map that traced previous mergers to show the historical logic that led to this moment, which was labeled "Growing Together." By demonstrating the similarities between the companies, Kraft showed that it understood and respected Cadbury.

You can apply this technique in your dealings with incumbents. Engage them as historians who can educate you on their history, a history you desire to understand. Don't wait for incumbents to call you out. Don't let them be able to honestly say you changed things without stopping to consider why they were being done differently before. Invite them to tell you the history first.

Psychologist and business writer Carol Dweck offers us the concept of a growth mindset over a fixed mindset. People with a growth mindset, she theorizes, believe that their talents can be developed, while people with a fixed mindset believe that their talents are inborn and can't be increased.[2] A growth mindset asks you to fight against your desire to avoid challenges, give up easily when there are obstacles, and easily feel threatened by others' success. A growth mindset helps you embrace challenges, persist in the face of setbacks, and be inspired by others' success. One way to recognize if you have a true growth mindset is your use of the term "failing." Try replacing that word with the word "learning."

Organizations with a growth mindset, Dweck notes, "encourage appropriate risk-taking, knowing that some risks won't work out. They reward employees for important and useful lessons learned, even if a project does not meet its original goals. They support collaboration across organizational boundaries rather than competition among employees or units. They are committed to the growth of every member . . . and they continually reinforce growth mindset values with concrete policies."[3]

This means, once you personally have a growth mindset, you can encourage others to go down the same path. For example, you may not be able to compliment incumbents' ideas, but you can compliment their engagement with you in a healthy, mature, and open way. Dweck calls this

continued

a process compliment. Its opposite, of course, equally useful in our minds, is a process criticism. If they choose not to attend the meeting or to write a nastily worded email, you can take issue not with their opinion but with their tact. You can invite them to engage, and, if they do, focus again on process to reinforce that you value when they contribute, even if they disagree. Either way, you are inspiring their focus on growth and ability to change. And even if they're not going to become great partners, you've learned a lot about how they think and work.

Be aware, however, that even as historians, incumbents may not have your best interests in mind (more on this in the next chapter). This is critical. See if you can align their entrenched interests with your desire to innovate and drive innovation. It is possible that you'll be a threat to them, and they will do much to stop you. Yet you may be able to help them reach new markets because of your agility, for example. The goal may be to partner with or sell your company to the incumbents so they don't oppose you. There's a long history of larger incumbents purchasing smaller, more creative upstarts. For example, Unilever, one of the largest food companies in the world, purchased Ben & Jerry's. Coca-Cola purchased Honest Tea. Colgate purchased Tom's of Maine. These larger companies are interested in the markets served by these smaller niche brands. They recognize that it would be nearly impossible for them to innovate in ways that would allow them to be successful in these niche markets. So they acquire the talent, access to markets, and customers they see as necessary for building future profitability.

Even with all the reorienting you attempt to make people and institutions who could be villains into allies, there is only so much you can expect. They may still act in opposition to your work. Part of protecting a unified vision is recognizing the potential for damaging maneuvers that could come from where you, actually, least expect them.

CHAPTER 30

Managing Secret Agendas

· ·

A harsh reality exists: while most intersection environments are built on honesty, transparency, and disclosure, sometimes these may not serve the work you are trying to accomplish. We are *not* suggesting that you engage in dishonest activity, but we *are* suggesting that it is important to be careful with how much you share and when. Private-sector workers are used to working with significant amounts of secrecy and nondisclosure agreements. But because ventures operating at the intersection of sectors and public-sector work often demand transparency and public disclosure, absolute secrecy is not possible.

One insight from our research was that threats to the intersection from dissenters and incumbents often came by hiding or obscuring relevant details and revealing truth only partially. Some potential partners will say one thing in public and do another thing in private. This can be hard to figure out. There is only one person you can reliably practice on to learn the skills necessary to do this and recognize it in others—yourself. What, exactly, are you hiding . . . from yourself? Robert Kegan and Lisa Lahey call this your immunity to change.[1] The concept is that we all, at some level, work to protect ourselves from a failure to make lasting change. We want to keep that New Year's resolution. We know it's good for us, and we say we are going to do it. But we never do. We lie to ourselves all the time. Learning to recognize this in yourself can help you recognize it in others.

Practicing managing secret agendas

1. Commitment	2. Doing/Not Doing	3. Hidden Competing Commitments	4. Big Assumptions
We are committed to completing and publishing our book.	1. We are prioritizing our direct client consultant work. 2. We are spending time with our families. 3. We are not exploring options for self- or hybrid publishing. 4. We are focusing on projects where we have project managers to schedule our time.	1. (We fear falling behind.) We are committed to not letting our colleagues down. 2. (We fear being seen as workaholics.) We are committed to showing our priorities are in the right place. 3. (We fear our work is not good enough.) We are committed to being perfect. 4. (We fear how much time this all will really take.) We are committed to treating this as an independent side project from our more pressing concerns.	1. If we prioritize a book that will only indirectly benefit our business, our colleagues will feel we don't respect their needs. 2. If we spend less time with our families, they will think we don't value them as much. 3. If we produce something that is not our 100 percent effort or isn't tremendously commercially successful, we won't be proud of it. 4. If the process of finalizing and publishing the book is more time intensive than we realized, it will feel like it wasn't worth doing in the first place.

Kegan and Lahey break it down into four simple brainstorming columns in what they call an immunity X-ray: commitment, doing/not doing, hidden competing commitments, and big assumptions.[2] Let's say your goal is to lose weight. In the first column, you write your commitment to lose weight. In the second, you write your "fearless inventory" of what you are actively doing to not meet that commitment, like your snacking and your unused gym membership. In the third column, you list your hidden competing commitments, like to those big meals where you spend quality time with your family and to keeping your reputation as a foodie with your friends. In the last column, you brainstorm the assumptions that are hiding within all this, such as you won't fit in anymore with your loved ones and your friends will no longer think you are interesting.

As an example, we thought about our "immunity to change" as we worked to finish this book. Here is what we found.

➡ COMMITMENT

We are committed to completing and publishing our book.

➡ IMMUNITY TO CHANGE #1

Doing/Not Doing Instead

We are prioritizing our direct client consultant work.

Hidden Competing Commitments

We are committed to not letting our colleagues down.
(We fear falling behind.)

Big Assumptions

If we prioritize a book that will only indirectly benefit our
business, our colleagues will feel we don't respect their needs.

➡ IMMUNITY TO CHANGE #2

Doing/Not Doing Instead

We are spending time with our families.

Hidden Competing Commitments

We are committed to showing our priorities are in
the right place. (We fear being seen as workaholics.)

Big Assumptions

If we spend less time with our families, they will think
we don't value them as much.

➡ IMMUNITY TO CHANGE #3

Doing/Not Doing Instead

We are not exploring options for self- or hybrid publishing.

Hidden Competing Commitments

We are committed to being perfect.
(We fear our work is not good enough.)

Big Assumptions

If we produce something that is not our 100 percent effort
or isn't tremendously commercially successful, we won't be
proud of it.

continued

➡ IMMUNITY TO CHANGE #4

Doing/Not Doing Instead

We are focusing on projects where we have project managers
to schedule our time.

Hidden Competing Commitments

We are committed to treating this as an independent side
project from our more pressing concerns. (We fear how much
time this all will really take.)

Big Assumptions

If the process of finalizing and publishing the book is more
time intensive than we realized, it will feel like it wasn't
worth doing in the first place.

You will never truly know what secrets others choose not to share,
but using a tool like this helps you understand the possibilities that might
lie beneath. Obscuring details from someone else is an option you may
have to take, but following a hunch of what might actually be behind their
desire to shake the foundation of the unity is a potentially much stronger
one. You may even try to write out an immunity X-ray for your partners.
In that way, you will uncover secret agendas your partners may have. You
will also understand what you, and they, have to lose by coming together
in this coalition.

Once you have used this tool to see where your secrets are, you can
create some experiments to see if your assumptions are correct. Following our earlier rules on experimentation, which are actually adapted from
none other than Kegan and Lahey, you can experiment in very low-stakes
ways to feel safe and gradually expand from there. You can honestly test
yourself, though you are probably correct to assume that many of the
assumptions are false. You will still be loved and thought of as interesting,
even if you lose some weight. Those elements may be expressed differently,
but they will still be there.

In an ideal world, you convince your collaborators to conduct this exercise and readily share the results. In the real world, you will both be able to have your guard up against secret agendas and be more empathetic to them. Much as you design small experiments for yourself to test your assumptions, you can design small experiments to test your assumptions about others. For instance, just try asking someone, "It feels like _____ may be something worth exploring. Do you think that's important?" Most people will come clean or, possibly, even recognize for the first time that they are feeling something, if it is simply just mentioned to them.

Manage secret agendas by awareness, empathy, and a willingness to learn. Do it consistently and fairly with your allies and your potential plotters. Call on the system, network, and movement skills you've built along the way and your ability to see and analyze all perspectives. Hold yourself to the same standards; recognize that you are pursuing a secret agenda as well and seek to engage it.

If you somehow manage to do all of this, the intersection will feel to others one day like it just magically came together. You will know better. In theater, we say, "The audience only knows what you allow them to see." It can be total chaos backstage, but the moment you step out on that stage, you present a polished product that comes from the collaborative energies of so many, each playing their part.

But to borrow another, more well-known phrase, "The show must go on."

CHAPTER 31

Building a Biotechnology Start-Up through Science and Regulation

This case is based on Dr. Lorin Johnson, founder of Salix Pharmaceuticals. We met with him to discuss his experiences in transitioning from academic research to developing a successful pharmaceutical enterprise. The quotes are taken from an interview in May 2021.

Certain industries know that you need to be able to harness the power of business, government, and the nonprofit sector working collaboratively. The biotech industry is undoubtedly one of those. Scientific knowledge, business intelligence, political acumen, and community connections are needed to develop and deploy products at scale. Many outsiders to the industry don't understand the complex regulatory hurdles needed to bring innovations to the marketplace. Further, nonprofits and community groups provide essential connections and community knowledge to ensure that the medications reach the most vulnerable people. The recent pandemic is a potential example—while many vaccines were delivered through medical offices, many more were delivered through nonprofit community clinics, pop-up events, and community-based health workers.

Salix Pharmaceuticals and its founder Lorin Johnson are great studies in the principles discussed in this book because they took an unconventional pathway to getting their idea to the marketplace. Your standard biotechnology company starts with a platform technology or a university professor generating research, and they generate early seed funding to organize a corporate structure and hire a few people to do some experiments. Usually a drug hasn't been identified. They know what experiments need to be done, but they need funding for basic research before they ever dream of a product.

Johnson, as an academic scientist with little track record in business or industry connections, needed to try new approaches. Salix Pharmaceuticals started by in-licensing a product that had already been through phase two, in which trials have already revealed a drug is safe and works for a particular condition it is meant to combat. In-licensing allows one company to take on some of the risk, and some of the reward, of a product being developed in another company. For an industry with a deep history of mergers and acquisitions, this mitigates the risk of taking on another company's less-appealing technologies.

Salix Pharmaceuticals knew what had been spent on their product. They knew what had to be spent to get it to market. But what Johnson and his cofounder, Randy Hamilton, had was *too* real. Rather than energizing a funding base through the untapped potential of a dreamer, they were weighed down by the fundamental clarity and reality of raw science. Investors like to shoot for the moon; they like big ideas with unlimited potential. Salix was just trying to help people suffering from inflammatory bowel disease. You could more or less accurately estimate what its market potential was, and it was going to be strong but not unlimited. While maintaining a clear path to earnings might have been seen as a good thing, this was not the type of inspirational pitch that got seed funding. Early on, they struggled to find investors.

Slowly but surely, they turned things around. How? By leading like a movement. But, as you've hopefully learned through the course of this book, they first had to think like a system and act like a network to get there. As we've discussed, you don't need anyone's permission to do this. For Lorin Johnson, this was simply how he built his career.

Think like a system

So how did Johnson become so skilled at licensing? "I am a scientist," he told us, laughing. He received his PhD in 1976 and was a postdoc at UCSF from 1976 until 1980. Half of his fellow postdocs went to Genentech and Chiron, the Bay Area biotech darlings founded in the era, but Johnson decided to go into academic research. After serving in the faculty of pathology for three years, he wound up turning a 180 and leaving Stanford in 1983. His adviser had started a company called California Biotechnology that was part of what he identified as the "second wave" of start-up Silicon Valley biotech firms. He moved the same lab he was working on at the nonprofit university into the start-up world and "just kept working on inflammation."

Johnson's ability to observe with curiosity and recognize patterns and the emerging trends in research moving to the private sector led to this important moment of tapping into his intuition. He was able to stick to his focus on inflammation as a hard science but reframed it for a new way of seeing things to make what felt like a 180 at the time actually just become the next step on the ladder of his career.

Of course, this only put Johnson in the right place at the right time. He needed to use other levers to take advantage of this opportunity to build toward a movement he would one day lead.

Act like a network

California Biotechnology's business model was to clone the gene, express the protein, and file the patents, then turn to big pharma to do all the development, clinical trials, and production, leaving behind a royalty on a billion-dollar drug. "As soon as you became successful in the lab," Johnson reminded us, "business development is out on the road trying to sell your science. And the scientist has to go along. It turned out I was a good communicator about the science." Through getting out of his silo in trying to sell his science, Johnson learned another professional language in communicating his science through a business development lens. In fact, he became the director of scientific operations, and when business development went on the road, he would code-mix to talk about the full portfolio of products available to be licensed.

Johnson met his business partner through working with the business development department in California Biotechnology. They assigned Randy Hamilton to focus on Japan in the height of its economic prosperity in the 1980s. After success for half a decade, they realized they could do this . . . on their own. "Science is my business, and business is my hobby," Johnson told us. "And my partner was exactly the opposite."

But, actually, "you can*not* do it on your own," he added.

"Out of necessity, when you don't have staff in regulatory or in clinical, and you have an asset and all of a sudden you have enough money to run a phase three clinical study, you've got to learn how to do it. So, I did! . . . When you are a molecular biologist, you don't even learn statistics. So, my business partner had his basic statistics books from college." Using his academic background at UCSF, he connected to the most famous gastroenterologist in the world, Marvin Sleisenger, MD, to be one of his first investors. He was understanding hidden power, recognizing that it was not just how much funds an investor could provide but also the doors they could open. "And he opened doors all over the world for us." He lined up all the investigators through people he knew and had trained around the United States.

Lead like a movement

So what do you do when you have scientist investors with good connections, but venture capitalists turn their backs? You have to integrate multiple logics and find a different business route. You think about the skills you have—and Johnson might not have had success with pitching, but one world he knew inside and out was licensing agreements. So Salix took their worldwide rights and looked . . . worldwide. Licensing the product outside the United States to other pharmaceutical companies brought in seed investment, and a variety of other sources kept them afloat, including Small Business Innovation Research federal grants. Had the patient advocacy group, the nonprofit Crohn's & Colitis Foundation, been as big as it is today, they would likely have funded it as well. But, according to Johnson, the market then was $150 million. It is $6 billion now.

One formidable new area of learning was the Food and Drug Administration (FDA). So they decided that the best way to establish feedback loops to learn how to work with them was to make the FDA their first customer. And they learned "on the fly." They "tell you what language they want you to speak" and they give you a checklist of things you have to have done. "It doesn't matter if you bring in a Nobel Prize winner. In fact, that's a kiss of death; don't do that," he raised to us. To manage this dissonance, Johnson took an approach reminiscent of how David Emerald reoriented the Drama Triangle into The Empowerment Dynamic. The victim becomes the creator. The persecutor becomes the challenger. "They are calling the shots, and you just respond to them. With good science," he added, "if you approach with lawyers and bully tactics, your stuff is going on the bottom of the pile.

"You have to develop a relationship—it's the same in business partnerships; you make a relationship first." This is a trick of managing incumbents, and there are no greater incumbents than the regulators who have seen every type of product try to make it through their screens. Johnson was able to build a relationship in which he showed he valued

202 DON'T LEAD ALONE

their history and perspective. He recognized the FDA's medical reviewers had an exceptional breadth of knowledge and there was no cutting corners to what they had to pace through to approve a drug.

Managing secret agendas

Interestingly, Johnson currently owns a venture capital company, Glycyx, which now almost exclusively acquires products that have been through phase two research. Once again, he is going the untraditional path. He shared with us an interesting insight about his current work that speaks to our final *Lead Like a Movement* section skill: *Managing Secret Agendas*.

We spoke briefly about the COVID-19 pandemic. "Vaccine development is not very sexy for a company until there is a pandemic and then it's too late," Johnson added. "The steps were not difficult. Someone just needed to pay for it . . . [and] big pharma is not going to pay for it if there is not a return for their shareholders. That's just the way it is. . . . There's this dichotomy between what we need to do and what companies will finance themselves."

In academics, you get funding based on where there is a need for science. Business, without regulation, in an industry with human lives at stake, should not be the answer unto itself. A workaround Johnson has discovered is quite interesting. While an insurance company's costs go down if a patient dies sooner, the military acts by opposite rules. They want their soldiers back in the field as quickly and as healthy as possible. He often turns to them as critical buyers to further his products. This is a real-life result that uses the same tools as Kegan and Lahey's "immunity to change."[1] Johnson thought about what his buyers were truly committed to—and for big pharma that is a return to its shareholders over a need for science. Understanding that this is what makes them immune to change, he looked toward the hidden agenda of the military and noticed a different system at work that served his needs.

Conclusion

Johnson and Hamilton were so poor at first, that while sitting in their first office (outside the second bedroom in Hamilton's house), one of their consultants on the business side had gone to J.P. Morgan in San Francisco and came back and said, "I figured out what we are! We are a *virtual* company." The year was 1993. They barely had networks yet, and the internet was just starting to be truly searchable. In 2015, they sold the company for $15 billion. It is now the biggest profit center for a parent company, Bausch Health, all the while creating medicines that help manage devastating medical conditions like ulcerative colitis and hepatic encephalopathy, which causes liver failure, coma, and death.

The value of recognizing his role in the system, building a network for himself and his business, and leading like a movement in motivating diverse stakeholders to help him achieve his goals has clearly led to great financial success for Johnson. But the true success of intersection work is the benefit it has for everyone else too.

The Open Road

. . . .

Once you have learned how to think like a system, act like a network, and lead like a movement, it is time to move through the intersection and onto the open road. We've covered a lot on our journey together. You will be tempted to just roll down the windows, blast the radio, and activate cruise control.

Before you get too excited, we want to leave you with a couple of cautions that make working at the intersection harder than it already sounds. Think about the last time you drove on a highway. There are external forces: Heavy winds. Potholes. Tractor trailers drifting a little too close for comfort. There are internal forces: Backseat drivers. Texting while driving. Failing to check blind spots. So just like the open road perhaps seems easier than it is, even when everything is set up, consensus is gained, and you've built a new system at an intersection that is functioning at a high level, there are things to watch out for.

With that in mind, we wanted to warn you of some traps to avoid after the work is "complete" (we trust you are smart enough to know the work is *never* complete).

1. The complacency blind spot

Economist Tyler Cowen's 2017 book, *The Complacent Class: The Self-Defeating Quest for the American Dream*, restates the American Dream as "life with not much change, where you get to keep what you feel is yours." He points out that start-ups, as a percentage of total business, have been declining since the 1980s. Dominated by big business, the innovation of Silicon Valley has been adapted less and less for motivational societal breakthroughs and more for convenience and leisurely screen time that keep consumers sated. Indeed, Cowen particularly notices how we are de-emphasizing advances in the physical world in favor of advances in the world of information. We are reminded of the Pixar film *WALL-E*, where humanity has been evacuated to a spaceship run by a company humorously called Buy-n-Large and has grown so complacent to convenience and screens that people have become massively overweight and unable to care for themselves. As the Internet of Things starts us down the path of technology easing our home lives, it's pretty scary that Cowen thinks we have taken a step in that direction (though you can argue Pixar does too or else they wouldn't have come up with the idea in the first place).

Of course, in the few years since he published his book, there has been a rise in some of the acts of physical un-complacency Cowen thought were disappearing, notably protests and civil disobedience, for which, interestingly, information technology has played a vital and active role. It points out a harsh but hopeful reality. Complacency is still, ultimately, a choice. Once you've found your right partners and formed your intersection, it's easy to no longer feel it necessary to get out of your silo, because you assume it's now balanced with the perspectives of others. The word "complacent," after all, comes from the Latin "complacēre," meaning "to please."[1] It is our human nature to want to think a task is done. To relax into our success. If we surround ourselves with an echo chamber of pleasure as to what we created, then something like social media serves as a language of meaninglessness, typewritten noise distributed and consumed by our silos. If you succumb to the echo chamber, you may miss warning signs that your intersection project needs to continue to evolve to meet new or previously undiscovered needs as they arise. However, if you choose to keep questioning and opening your mind to new ideas, that un-complacency can be a tool for systems thinking, network activation, and movement leadership that brings together partners to better solve or address new problems.

 Practicing avoiding the complacency blind spot

To avoid this blind spot, we suggest a tool from factory and construction zone work, where growing complacent can literally be life or death. A "toolbox talk" is an informal group discussion on a safety issue that aims to encourage workers to always be vigilant and forward-thinking about what could go wrong before it happens, prior to a daily shift starting. In its toolbox talk on workplace complacency, the Newfoundland & Labrador Construction and Safety Association instructs workers to ask the following before they begin work:[2]

➡ WHO AND WHAT ARE YOU WORKING WITH?

➡ WHAT WILL YOU BE DOING?

➡ WHERE WILL YOU BE GOING?

➡ WHAT MAY HAVE CHANGED?

➡ WHAT COULD GO WRONG?

These simple but easy-to-skip questions can also be used for facing down the complacency that may arise in your intersection workplace. You are likely a new person, with new allies and new capabilities. As you move forward, your need to check your blind spots will feel less necessary; on the contrary, it will have never been more important. If you are a lone worker having another day on a job you have done a thousand times before, we can understand the urge to grow complacent. If you are engaging in overlapping systems, complex networks, and dynamic movements, it is total fallacy to assume anything but change.

2. The distracting backseat driver

Another fallacy that is easy to assume is that your confidence in yourself to navigate the open road will be infallible once you have succeeded in something as complex as intersection work. There will be two strong backseat driver voices of doubt that prove otherwise quickly.

You are now driving with allies you didn't have before, and if your job has been done well, their voices will be nurtured to an extent that they trust you to take them to your next destination, whether you've invited them or not. Like the board game The Game of Life, your car will just get fuller and fuller of little plastic player pieces.

DETOUR: What The Game of Life teaches us about the game of life

The choice of this metaphor is not coincidental. While the 1960 release of The Game of Life, which took the same basic form of today's version, invokes the suburban American Dream of marrying, having 2.3 children, and owning a home with a picket fence (hopefully in Millionaire Acres), it was actually a 100th anniversary remake of the first board game ever designed by the company's namesake, Milton Bradley.

The original 1860 version ended in Happy Old Age, a much more modest goal for a more modest period. It also acknowledged some harsh realities, even with an option to land in Suicide. More likely, you would hit Honesty,

Bravery, or Success along the way or Poverty, Idleness, or Disgrace. Bradley claimed to have "invented a New Social Game,"[3] but it likely descended from centuries of games like Jñāna Chaupār ("game of knowledge"), where you could land on a square to climb a ladder to the god Vishnu or, alternatively, get swallowed by a snake. Another predecessor, the New Game of Human Life, was available in the late 18th century in England and soon came to America. It had 84 squares, one for each year of a person's life. A game called The Mansion of Happiness was quite successful in the years leading up to Bradley's "invention," with the title a suggestion of the final destination of heaven.

The difference in Bradley's original design, however, and perhaps what made it so lasting, was the choices you had to make along the way. In the early version, for instance, you decided whether to risk trying to get a secondary education, which could land you in poverty if you rolled the wrong number. The 1960's incarnation likewise offered the choice between going to college or directly into business. Interestingly, this was practically the only choice that remained in the remake. Instead of life being a battle between good and bad choices, it hinged on an early decision and then took you through a series of random occurrences and small resulting choices.

While you will see that these two types of the game map nicely to the two different backseat drivers we introduce below, this is also an example of recombinant innovation, a concept we presented way back in our authors' note. Bradley made something wholly original, but it was not, on the whole, original. It borrowed and adapted the best ideas that came before and around it. We hope you recognize this approach as a through line to all the skills we have introduced that allow you to think like a system, act like a network, and lead like a movement. No good work is done in a vacuum.

The first of the two different backseat drivers is the one who effectively acts as a copilot. They stay with you from the kinds of intersection decisions you have to make early that will begin to earn you followers and allies. They are, mostly, welcome. You want them in your car. They believe in you and can see what you do. They can also look out for things you can't. They have learned how to ask the right questions when you need them, which brings a burden to your ability to just instinctually trust your new skills, sure, but you can count on your ability to think like a system to find the answers.

The second backseat driver actually comes from within: it's self-doubt. In the great song "Die Vampire, Die!" from the musical *[title of show]* (yes, the title of this musical is actually *[title of show]* . . . it's meta), Susan Blackwell relates to the audience that the "mother of all vampires" is self-despair—thinking you will never be good enough. "Why is it if some dude walked up to me on the subway platform," she opines, "and said these things, I would think he was a mentally ill asshole, but if the vampire inside my head says it, it's the voice of reason."

It is a fallacy to think that the road ahead will not be as riddled with self-doubt as the road you took to get to the intersection. It does not play out like The Game of Life with its brightly colored plastic pieces and over-simplified questions and outcomes. It is full of important decisions and a bigger challenge than listening to the doubts and questions of the external backseat drivers you picked up a while back (more like the 1860's version of the game). Instead, they will gnaw at your confidence from inside your own head, even as you have proven yourself capable of working this all out.

The answer? Milton Bradley once wrote that "the journey of life is governed by a combination of chance and judgment."[4] There is a lot of modern literature on how people make their own luck by putting them-selves in a position to get lucky. But, we argue, they still ultimately have to *get lucky.* Just because you don't follow up one success with another imme-diately doesn't mean you have to doubt yourself. It's not about always being successful. It's about what you do with the good luck once you get it. Once you've done the work to see outside the blinds of your silo, you can have confidence in the decisions you make, regardless of outcome.

You are a courageous penguin. Sometimes there are just unseen things in the water. Thus we reach the final trap we want to warn you about on the open road.

3. The unseen pothole

Like with any good entrepreneur or intrapreneur, we trust you will be making small, creative experiments, switching from lane to lane, speeding up and slowing down, and occasionally even hitting cruise control to enjoy a stretch for a little. You can do this without complacency by paying attention to what may have changed and thinking about what could go wrong. You can do this without being distracted by the backseat driver, invited or uninvited.

But there are some things you just can't see coming. Weather events are a great example of this—natural disasters can destroy or seriously disrupt infrastructure that partnerships have carefully built over decades. We tend to look back and chide ourselves for not seeing this coming. We mourn the mistakes that were made and vow not to do it again, but then . . . it happens anyway.

Brené Brown has a great answer for this. The researcher, storyteller, and professor has introduced some interesting ideas around the story we tell ourselves versus the reality of what happened. On the road, we blame everything that happens on external circumstances. "That person cut me off!" "They need to fix the roads!" In real life, however, we tend to do the opposite. If, say, your partner cheats on you, you might frequently tell a story of what *you* are doing wrong that led to this "fall." To recover from this, Brown speaks of having to go through three phases: reckoning, rumble, and revolution.[5] The idea behind reckoning is to walk into your own story and examine and uncover the emotions you are having. You don't need to interrogate yourself; instead, be mindful and listen to what your body is physically telling you in its reaction. In the rumble, she recommends writing your messy first draft to be able to see on paper the complex emotions you are feeling. The revolution calls on you to then rewrite your story with the ending you actually want.

In other words, there are consequences to *Daring Greatly*, the title of her best-selling book on how being courageous enough to be vulnerable can transform your life. *Rising Strong*, her book that introduces these acts of recovery, was written in response. After publishing *Daring Greatly*, she said that "my team and I have . . . received emails every week from people who write, 'I dared greatly. I got my butt kicked and now I'm down for the count. How do I get back up?'"[6] Instead of focusing on the fallacy that we could have done something differently in the past in a situation that was out of our control, Brown is shifting our mindset to think about getting up and trying again and writing another story. Often, at intersections, this means literally rebuilding with new protections in place and new collaborators brought in that can fill in the skills that were not previously there. You may find that your initial intersection work is only one piece of the puzzle.

We are reminded of the serenity prayer, popular in 12-step programs, in which the supplicant asks a higher power to give them "the courage to change the things I can." An earlier version of the prayer, however, starts, "Oh, God, give us courage to change what must be altered."[7] We prefer this version for our purposes, as it asks for courage not to change what you can but what you *must*. The pothole may not be your fault, but it is your responsibility to recover from the bump. With the skills you've learned from this book, we're confident you can.

We're excited to hear about your journey. As practitioners and writers, we're always learning, and we usually learn the most from our clients and readers. We are convinced that the world needs this intersection work. We don't need better nonprofits, corporations, and governments; we need the human power to see across divides and make things happen. You don't need to lead alone. We are in this together, even if sometimes we can't see it.

Please stay in touch.

Acknowledgments

· ·

Shocking as it may be for a book titled *Don't Lead Alone* . . . we didn't do this alone.

We'd like to thank our many clients over the years and the entire team at Potrero Group, especially our amazing managing director Andrew Leider, who constantly teaches us what it means to lead together. We also particularly want to thank Rhia Bordon, who, as an MPA intern in New York and then continuing as an associate consultant all the way from Germany, provided critical supplementary research, edits, and citations.

We have both been guided by incredible academic and professional mentors, many of them from UC Davis Graduate School of Management. Being located adjacent to the seat of government of the world's fifth largest economy and the heart of innovation, Silicon Valley, creates a unique laboratory for exploring the ideas in this book. A big shout-out goes to Dr. Andrew Hargadon, who served as Cleve's PhD adviser, mentor, and supervisor at the UC Davis Institute for Innovation and Entrepreneurship. Drs. Nicole Biggart, Chris Benner, and Greg Moore invested deeply in Cleve and profoundly shaped his academic and professional trajectory.

We worked with incredible people who helped us shape the voice of this book. Alexandra Hammond helped us begin to visualize the book from a designer's eye. Check her out at alexhammondstudio.com. The book took shape under the watchful eye of a patient and encouraging developmental editor named Erin Brenner. Find her services at righttouchediting.com. And, of course, the entire team at Greenleaf, but particularly our editor

Morgan Robinson and project manager Jen Glynn. They taught us if you invest in quality for your first book, you get quality.

A special thanks to Cleve's students over the years, especially those from UC Davis's Executive Leadership Program, one of whom took our just-OK title and re-proposed it as *Don't Lead Alone* (we won't embarrass ourselves and tell you all the bad versions of that we came up with on a particularly punchy Friday afternoon). Speaking of UC Davis, some of these ideas in this book were researched and developed as we built our Coursera specialization, Management of Multinational and Cross-Cultural Teams. Jacob Hosier oversaw the development of our curriculum and was our thought partner for our content, while Jennifer Kremer went above and beyond project management to elevate our final product beyond what we possibly could have expected. Go to www.coursera.org/specializations/management-multinational-cross-cultural-teams to see our mutual hard work.

We'd like to thank our families and many friends and colleagues. Daniel's parents, Adina and Sharon, are his constant cheerleaders, trusted advisers, and lifelong educators. His wife, Jiaxuan, unflinchingly supported the time and expense it took to make this dream of writing a book a reality, but also dedicated countless hours and deep wisdom to help think about and refine everything from the overall structure of the book to the title. Cleve would like to shout out to his dear children, Galen and Daniel, who are his North Star. His brothers Robert and Thomas and his sister Paige have always been there for him and provided a deep comfort and grounding through life's journey.

Finally, thanks go to you, our reader. We wrote this for you, and keeping you in mind helped us through the many challenges of seeing a book through to completion. We hope that the ideas we've shared here, most of which we learned from others, prove useful to you as you work to make a better world. Please stay in touch and tell us about your journey!

Leadership and Change Management Resources

· ·

Ajaz Ahmed, *Limitless: Leadership That Endures*
(London: Ebury Publishing, 2015).

Warren Bennis, *On Becoming a Leader*
(New York: Basic Books, 2009).

M. L. Chibber, *Sai Baba's Mahavakya on Leadership*
(New Delhi: M&M International Publishers, 1995).

Yvon Chouinard, *Let My People Go Surfing*
(London: Penguin Books, 2006).

Jim Collins, *Good to Great*
(New York: Random House, 2001).

Chip Conley, *Peak: How Great Companies Get Their Mojo from Maslow*
(United Kingdom: Wiley, 2007).

Mihály Csíkszentmihályi, *Good Business:
Leadership, Flow, and the Making of Meaning*
(London: Penguin Books, 2004).

Angela Duckworth, *Grit: The Power of Passion and Perseverance*
(New York: Scribner, 2016).

Carol S. Dweck, PhD, *Mindset: The New Psychology of Success*
(New York: Random House, 2006).

Ranulph Fiennes, *Shackleton*
(New York: Pegasus Books, 2022).

Seth Godin, *Tribes: We Need You to Lead Us*
(United Kingdom: Little, Brown Book Group, 2011).

Ronald Heifetz, Alexander Grashow, and Marty Linsky,
*The Practice of Adaptive Leadership: Tools and Tactics for
Changing Your Organization and the World*
(Boston: Harvard Business School Publishing, 2009).

Frances Hesselbein and Marshall Goldsmith, eds., *The Leader
of the Future 2: Visions, Strategies, and Practices for the New*
(New Jersey: Wiley, 2006).

John Kotter, *Leading Change*
(Boston: Harvard Business Review Press, 2012).

James Kouzes and Barry Posner, *The Leadership Challenge:
How to Make Extraordinary Things Happen in Organizations*, 6th ed.
(New Jersey: Wiley, 2017).

Frederic LaLoux, *Reinventing Organizations:
A Guide to Designing Meaningful Organizations*
(Brussels: Nelson Parker, 2014).

Anne Lamott, *Bird by Bird*
(New York: Anchor Publishing, 1995).

Richard Leider, *The Power of Purpose*
(California: Berrett-Koehler Publishers, 2015).

George Leonard, *Mastery*
(London: Penguin Books, 1991).

Rue Mapp, *Nature Swagger:*
Stories and Visions of Black Joy in the Outdoors
(San Francisco: Chronicle Books, 2022).

Dan Pink, *Drive*
(New York: Riverhead Books, 2011).

Amanda Ripley, *High Conflict*
(New York: Simon & Schuster, 2021).

Sheryl Sandberg, *Lean In: Women, Work, and the Will to Lead*
(United Kingdom: Ebury Publishing, 2013).

Peter M. Senge, *The Fifth Discipline*
(London: Random House, 2010).

Elizabeth Wiseman, *Multipliers:*
How the Best Leaders Make Everyone Smarter
(New York: HarperCollins, 2010).

Julie Zhuo, *The Making of a Manager:*
What to Do When Everyone Looks to You
(London: Ebury Publishing, 2019).

Notes

CHAPTER 1

1. Horst W. J. Rittel and Melvin M. Webber, "Dilemmas in a General Theory of Planning," *Policy Sciences* 4, no. 2 (June 1973): 155–69, doi: 10.1007/BF01405730.

2. Lu Wei Tan, "The Fascinating Science of Bubbles, from Soap to Champagne," TED Talk, December 17, 2018, 14:08, https://www.ted.com/talks/li_wei_tan_the_fascinating_science_of_bubbles_from_soap_to_champagne?language=enn.

3. "The Cleanest Line," Patagonia, https://www.patagonia.com/stories/.

4. "Yvon Chouinard," 1% for the Planet, https://www.onepercentfortheplanet.org/yvon-chouinard.

5. "Tin Shed Ventures: Funding the Next Generation of Responsible Businesses," Patagonia, https://www.patagonia.com/stories/tin-shed-ventures-funding-the-next-generation-of-responsible-businesses/story-31127.html.

6. Catherine Morin, "Patagonia's Customer Base and the Rise of an Environmental Ethos," CRM.org, June 24, 2020, https://crm.org/articles/patagonias-customer-base-and-the-rise-of-an-environmental-ethos.

7. Cleveland Justis, "Hybrid Organizing: Case Studies of Skills and Attributes Used to Generate Impact when Working at the Intersection of Sectors" (PhD diss., University of California, Davis, 2019), ProQuest 22622900.

8. "Alcatraz at a Glance," Golden Gate National Parks Conservancy, https://www.parksconservancy.org/our-work/alcatraz-glance; Nathan Hale Sargent, "Bay Area National Parks Generated $1 Billion in Economic Benefit to Local Communities in 2016," National Park Service, April 20, 2017, https://www.nps.gov/goga/learn/news/bay-area-national-parks-generate-1-billion-in-economic-benefit.htm.

9. Matthew Niksa, "Urban Confluence Picks 'Breeze of Innovation' as Winning Design for San Jose's New Light Tower," *Silicon Valley Business Journal*, March 25, 2021, https://www.bizjournals.com/sanjose/news/2021/03/25/urban-confluence-san-jose-light-tower-competition.html.

10. Michael E. Porter, "How Competitive Forces Shape Strategy," *Harvard Business Review* (March–April 1979), https://hbr.org/1979/03/how-competitive-forces-shape-strategy.

11. Michael E. Porter and Mark R. Kramer, "Creating Shared Value: How to Reinvent Capitalism—and Unleash a Wave of Innovation and Growth," *Harvard Business Review* (January–February 2011), http://www.relativimpact.com/downloads/HBR-Shared-value.pdf.

12. Geoff Kendall, "Is Your SDG Response Defensive, Selective or Holistic?," *Sustainable Brands* (June 15, 2020), https://sustainablebrands.com/read/marketing-and-comms/is-your-sdg-response-defensive-selective-or-holistic.

13. Kendall, "Is Your SDG Response Defensive, Selective or Holistic?"

CHAPTER 3

1. Peter Senge, "Navigating Webs of Interdependence," uploaded by A&S, April 26, 2017, https://youtu.be/WqxeLhKuEF0.

2. Kenneth Mikkelsen and Harold Jarche, "The Best Leaders Are Constant Learners," *Harvard Business Review* (October 16, 2015), https://hbr.org/2015/10/the-best-leaders-are-constant-learners.

3. Mikkelsen and Jarche, "The Best Leaders Are Constant Learners."

4. John Kania and Mark Kramer, "Collective Impact," *Stanford Social Innovation Review* 9, no. 1 (2011): 36–41. doi: 10.48558/5900-KN19.

5. Jane Wei-Skillern, Nora Silver, and Eric Heitz, "Cracking the Network Code: Four Principles for Grantmakers," *Grantmakers for Effective Organizations* (June 26, 2013), https://community-wealth.org/sites/clone.community-wealth.org/files/downloads/report-wei_skiller-et-al.pdf.

6. Kania and Kramer, "Collective Impact."

7. The Stakeholder Alignment Collaborative, "When Launching a Collaboration, Keep It Agile," *Stanford Social Innovation Review* 20, no. 2 (2022): 41–47.

8. Mara Cristina Caballero, "Academic Turns City into a Social Experiment," *Harvard Gazette*, March 11, 2004, https://news.harvard.edu/gazette/story/2004/03/academic-turns-city-into-a-social-experiment/.

9. "Bogotá, Colombia: Early Commitment to Safe and Active Transportation for Youth Still Going Strong," Vision Zero for Youth, https://www.visionzeroforyouth.org/stories/bogota-colombia/.

CHAPTER 4

1. Ludwig von Bertalanffy, "An Outline of General System Theory," *British Journal for the Philosophy of Science* 1, no. 2 (1950): 134–65, doi: 10.1093/bjps/I.2.134. See also "Systems Theory of Organization" (Harappa, May 17, 2021, https://harappa.education/harappa-diaries/systems-theory-of-organization) for a succinct summary of systems theory in organizations.

2. Christian Seelos and Johanna Mair, "Mastering System Change," *Stanford Social Innovation Review* 16, no. 4 (Fall 2018), https://ssir.org/articles/entry/mastering_system_change#.

CHAPTER 5

1. Francesca Gino, "The Business Case for Curiosity," *Harvard Business Review* (September–October 2018), https://hbr.org/2018/09/the-business-case-for-curiosity.

2. Curt Nickisch and Francesca Gino, "651: The Power of Curiosity," October 9, 2018, in *HBR IdeaCast*, produced by Mary Dooe, podcast, 28:56, https://hbr.org/podcast/2018/10/the-power-of-curiosity.

CHAPTER 6

1. "The Smith5Keys," Harold Smith System, https://www.drivedifferent.com/smith5keys/.

2. Christian Seelos and Johanna Mair, "Mastering System Change," *Stanford Social Innovation Review* 16, no. 4 (Fall 2018): 40, https://ssir.org/articles/entry/mastering_system_change#.

3. "Kurzweil Computer Products," *Kurzweil Technologies*, http://www.kurzweiltech.com/kcp.html.

4. Robert C. Barkman, "Why the Human Brain Is So Good at Detecting Patterns," *Psychology Today*, May 19, 2021, https://www.psychologytoday.com/us/blog/singular-perspective/202105/why-the-human-brain-is-so-good-detecting-patterns.

5. Alex Kantrowitz, "Use the 'Always Day One' Mindset to Power Innovation," interview by Skip Prichard, *Skip Prichard*, December 7, 2020, https://www.skipprichard.com/use-the-always-day-one-mindset-to-power-innovation/.

6. Jeff Bezos, "2016 Letter to Shareholders," Amazon.com, https://s2.q4cdn.com/299287126/files/doc_financials/annual/2016-Letter-to-Shareholders.pdf.

7. Larry Page and Sergey Brin, "2004 Founders' IPO Letter," Alphabet Investor Relations, https://abc.xyz/investor/founders-letters/2004-ipo-letter/.

8. Frederic Lardinois, "The Story behind Google's Cardboard Project," TechCrunch, June 26, 2014, https://techcrunch.com/2014/06/26/the-story-behind-googles-cardboard-project/.

9. Danielle LaBelle (@daniellabelle1), "If people did everything in a rush," Instagram, October 15, 2020, https://www.instagram.com/reel/CGYEf3Xj1ke/.

CHAPTER 7

1. Erin Gray, Madeline Tyson, and Charlie Bloch, "Systems Mapping: A Vital Ingredient for Successful Partnerships," *RMI*, August 17, 2020, https://rmi.org/systems-mapping-a-vital-ingredient-for-successful-partnerships/.

2. Christian Seelos and Johanna Mair, "Mastering System Change," *Stanford Social Innovation Review* 16, no. 4 (Fall 2018), https://ssir.org/articles/entry/mastering_system_change#.

CHAPTER 8

1. "Decoupling Policies," Center for Climate and Energy Solutions, updated March 2019, https://www.c2es.org/document/decoupling-policies/.

2. Souvik Datta, "Decoupling and Demand-Side Management: Evidence from the US Electric Industry," *Energy Policy* 132(C) (2019), 175–84, doi: 10.1016/j.enpol.2019.05.005.

CHAPTER 9

1. Leon Berg, "The Power of Listening—An Ancient Practice for Our Future," TEDx Talks, June 12, 2013, video, 17:02, https://youtu.be/6iDMuB6NjNA.

2. Guy Itzchakov and Avraham N. Kluger, "The Power of Listening in Helping People Change," *Harvard Business Review* (May 17, 2018), https://hbr.org/2018/05/the-power-of-listening-in-helping-people-change.

3. Shalvin Sunny, "5 Whys," *Six Sigma Study Guide*, https://sixsigmastudyguide.com/5-whys/.

4. Elyse Maltin, "What Successful Public-Private Partnerships Do," *Harvard Business Review* (January 8, 2019), https://hbr.org/2019/01/what-successful-public-private-partnerships-do.

CHAPTER 10

1. Laura Huang, "When It's OK to Trust Your Gut on a Big Decision," *Harvard Business Review* (October 22, 2019), https://hbr.org/2019/10/when-its-ok-to-trust-your-gut-on-a-big-decision.

CHAPTER 12

1. Revolution Foods, "Revolution Foods Urges Nation to Follow California in Permanently Adopting Free School Meals," PR Newswire, September 21, 2021, https://www.prnewswire.com/news-releases/revolution-foods-urges-nation-to-follow-california-in-permanently-adopting-free-school-meals-301380903.html.

CHAPTER 13

1. "How Many Solar Systems Are in Our Galaxy?," NASA Science, https://spaceplace.nasa.gov/other-solar-systems/en/.

2. Crockett Johnson, *Harold and the Purple Crayon* (New York: HarperCollins, 1992).

CHAPTER 14

1. "Liminal Leadership: An Exploration," *SYPartners*, https://vision.sypartners.com/2343117/.

2. "Harold Smith World Famous Driving Instructor Drifts into Lanes," uploaded by tubengagements, February 12, 2016, video, 8:23, https://youtu.be/1mYHss0Xmus.

3. Robert B. Zajonc, "Attitudinal Effects of Mere Exposure," *Journal of Personality and Social Psychology* 9, no. 2 (1968), doi: 10.1037/h0025848.

4. Jane Wei-Skillern, Nora Silver, and Eric Heitz, "Cracking the Network Code: Four Principles for Grantmakers," *Grantmakers for Effective Organizations* (June 26, 2013): 5, https://community-wealth.org/sites/clone.community-wealth.org/files/downloads/report-wei_skiller-et-al.pdf.

CHAPTER 15

1. Mara Cristina Caballero, "Academic Turns City into a Social Experiment," *Harvard Gazette*, March 11, 2004, https://news.harvard.edu/gazette/story/2004/03/academic-turns-city-into-a-social-experiment/.

2. Erin Meyer, *The Culture Map: Breaking Through the Invisible Boundaries of Global Business* (United States: PublicAffairs, 2014).

CHAPTER 17

1. Lisa M. Benton, *The Presidio: From Army Post to National Park* (Pennsylvania: Northeastern University Press, 1998).

2. See *The Presidio: From Army Post to National Park* by Lisa Benton or the *New Guardians of the Golden Gate: How America Got a Great National Park* by Amy Meyer for more detailed information on the Presidio's history.

3. The Presidio Trust was a case study explored in depth in Cleve's dissertation. For more information or to download a copy of the dissertation, please see https://www.proquest.com/openview/c275721ae6bac815baae6566bc772a03/1.pdf?pq-origsite=gscholar&cbl=18750&diss=y.

CHAPTER 18

1. Keegan-Michael Key and Jordan Peele, "Key & Peele—Obama Meet & Greet," Comedy Central, September 24, 2014, video, 1:54, https://youtu.be/nopWOC4SRm4.

CHAPTER 19

1. Mary Hayes et al., "The Global Study of Engagement Technical Report," *ADP Research Institute* (2019), https://www.adp.com/-/media/adp/ResourceHub/pdf/ADPRI/ADPRI0102_2018_Engagement_Study_Technical_Report_RELEASE%20READY.ashx.

2. Marcus Buckingham and Ashley Goodall, "The Power of Hidden Teams," *Harvard Business Review* (May 14, 2019), https://hbr.org/2019/05/the-power-of-hidden-teams.

3. A. Hyder, A. Blatt, A. D. Hollander, et al., "Design and Implementation of a Workshop for Evaluation of the Role of Power in Shaping and Solving Challenges in a Smart Foodshed," *Sustainability* 14, no. 5 (2022): 2642, https://doi.org/10.3390/su14052642.

4. Rob Cross and Laurence Prusak, "The People Who Make Organizations Go—or Stop," *Harvard Business Review* (June 2002), https://hbr.org/2002/06/the-people-who-make-organizations-go-or-stop.

CHAPTER 20

1. Vivian Glang, "This CEO Is Giving His Employees 'Get Out of Jail Free' Cards," Business Insider, March 20, 2013, https://www.businessinsider.com/this-ceo-is-giving-his-employees-get-out-of-jail-cards-free-cards-2013-3.

2. Leslie Kwoh, "Memo to Staff: Take More Risks," *Wall Street Journal*, March 20, 2013, https://www.wsj.com/articles/SB10001424127887323639604578370383939044780.

3. Randy Pausch, *The Last Lecture* (New York: Hyperion, 2008).

4. Pausch, *The Last Lecture*, 149.

CHAPTER 21

1. "Urban Development: Overview," World Bank, updated October 6, 2022, https://www.worldbank.org/en/topic/urbandevelopment/overview.

2. "History," Urban Sustainability Directors Network, accessed November 22, 2022, https://www.usdn.org/history.html.

3. Urban Sustainability Directors Network, "Strategic Vision and Plan 2022–2024," https://www.usdn.org/uploads/cms/documents/usdn_strategic_plan_22-24.pdf.

4. "Join," Urban Sustainability Directors Network, accessed November 22, 2022, https://www.usdn.org/join.html.

5. Kristin Baja, "Resilience Hubs: Shifting Power to Communities and Increasing Community Capacity," *Urban Sustainability Directors Network* (2018), https://www.usdn.org/uploads/cms/documents/usdn_resiliencehubs_2018.pdf.

6. Sadhu Aufochs Johnston, Steven S. Nicholas, and Julia Parzen, *The Guide to Greening Cities* (Washington, DC: Island Press, 2013).

7. USDN, "Strategic Vision and Plan 2022–2024"

8. USDN, "Strategic Vision and Plan 2022–2024"

9. "American Express Commits $5M to Help Cities Reduce Climate-Related Damage," Environment+Energy Leader, November 7, 2022, https://www.environmentalleader.com/2022/11/american-express-commits-5m-to-help-cities-reduce-climate-related-damage/.

CHAPTER 22

1. Neil J. Smelser, *Theory of Collective Behavior* (New York: Free Press, 1963).

2. John F. Kennedy, "Address at Rice University on the Nation's Space Effort, September 12, 1962," JFK Presidential Library and Museum, https://www.jfklibrary.org/archives/other-resources/john-f-kennedy-speeches/rice-university-19620912.

3. John F. Kennedy, "Address to the Joint Session of Congress, May 1961," JFK Presidential Library and Museum, https://www.jfklibrary.org/node/16986#:~:text=Speaking%20to%20Congress%20and%20the,National%20Aeronautic%20and%20Space%20Administration.

CHAPTER 23

1. Cory Stieg, "The Psychology behind a New iPhone Release—and Why It's So Hard to Resist," CNBC, December 8, 2020, https://www.cnbc.com/2020/12/08/the-psychology-of-new-iphone-releases-apple-marketing.html.

2. Ruud Wouters and Stefaan Walgrave, "What Makes Protest Powerful? Reintroducing and Elaborating Charles Tilly's WUNC Concept," *SSRN Electronic Journal* (February 1, 2017), doi: 10.2139/ssrn.2909740.

3. Benny C. Williams, "Martin Luther King Jr. Would Be So Pleased to See the People Who Have Been Protesting against Police Brutality," *Statesman Journal*, January 15, 2021, https://www.statesmanjournal.com/story/opinion/2021/01/15/martin-luther-king-jr-diversity-protesters-civil-rights-movement-guest-opinion/4184778001/.

4. Derek Sivers, "How to Start a Movement," TED, February 2010, video, 2:53, https://www.ted.com/talks/derek_sivers_how_to_start_a_movement/.

5. Werner Geyser, "35 Facebook Statistics—Revenue, Users," Influencer Marketing Hub, updated December 29, 2021, https://influencermarketinghub.com/facebook-statistics/.

CHAPTER 24

1. Brian Skerry, "The Culture of Whales," National Geographic, documentary, April 22, 2021, https://disneyplusoriginals.disney.com/show/secrets-of-the-whales.

2. Rosabeth Moss Kanter, "How Great Companies Think Differently," *Harvard Business Review* (November 2011), https://hbr.org/2011/11/how-great-companies-think-differently.

3. We like the template by Strategyzer ("The Business Model Canvas," Strategyzer, https://www.strategyzer.com/canvas/business-model-canvas), but you can use any template you like. SCORE has a free webinar on how to do one (Mark Lowenstein and Marc L. Goldberg, "An Easier Way to Prepare Your Business Plan—the Business Model Canvas," SCORE Association, October 24, 2019, recorded webinar, 45:00, https://www.score.org/event/an-easier-way-to-write-your-business-plan-the-business-model-canvas#.YgbTagmSUp8.link).

4. See the Community Toolbox website chapter on "Developing a Logic Model or Theory of Change" for a variety of tools and guidance about logic models. (See https://ctb.ku.edu/en/table-of-contents/overview/models-for-community-health-and-development/logic-model-development/main.)

CHAPTER 25

1. Jack Zenger and Joseph Folkman, "Overcoming Feedback Phobia: Take the First Step," *Harvard Business Review* (December 16, 2013), https://hbr.org/2013/12/overcoming-feedback-phobia-take-the-first-step.

CHAPTER 26

1. Simon Atkinson, "Airbnb Looks at Expanding into Leisure Activities," BBC News, May 5, 2016, https://www.bbc.com/news/technology-36212451.

2. John Hattie and Helen Timperley, "The Power of Feedback," *Review of Educational Research* 77, no. 81 (2007), doi: 10.3102/003465430298487.

3. Kindra Hall, "How the Founders of Airbnb Attracted Investors with a Story," *Leadership Essentials*, July 15, 2020, https://hcleadershipessentials.com/blogs/entrepreneurship/how-to-get-investors-with-story-like-airbnb.

4. Rebecca Aydin, "How 3 Guys Turned Renting Air Mattresses in Their Apartment into a $31 Billion Company, Airbnb," Business Insider, updated September 20, 2019, https://www.businessinsider.com/how-airbnb-was-founded-a-visual-history-2016-2.

5. Aydin, "How 3 Guys Turned Renting Air Mattresses."

6. Airbnb, "Opening Homes in Times of Crisis with Airbnb.org," Airbnb, December 7, 2020, https://www.airbnb.com/resources/hosting-homes/a/opening-homes-in-times-of-crisis-with-airbnborg-286.

CHAPTER 27

1. Keith H. Hammonds, "Michael Porter's Big Ideas," *Fast Company*, February 28, 2001, https://www.fastcompany.com/42485/michael-porters-big-ideas.

2. Satoru Iwata, *Ask Iwata: Words of Wisdom from Satoru Iwata, Nintendo's Legendary CEO* (United States: VizMedia, LLC, 2021).

3. This is also a good exercise for judging the value of the intersection project you're considering. Marketing guru Seth Godin has one version of the grid in which the axes are how big the positive outcome will be and how strong the chances of its success are. A project that lands in the upper-right quadrant is a project you want to be part of. (See more at Seth Godin, "A Simple 2x2 for Choices," *Seth's Blog*, January 1, 2021, https://seths.blog/2021/01/a-simple-quadrant-for-choices/.)

CHAPTER 28

1. Stephen B. Karpman, "Fairy Tales and Script Drama Analysis," *Transactional Analysis Bulletin* 7, no. 26 (1968): 39–43.

2. Stephen J. Dubner, "445: Why Do We Seek Comfort in the Familiar," December 23, 2020, in *No Stupid Questions*, produced by Rebecca Lee Douglas, podcast, 36:56, https://freakonomics.com/podcast/nsq-ep-30/.

CHAPTER 29

1. John T. Seaman Jr. and George David Smith, "Your Company's History as a Leadership Tool," *Harvard Business Review* (December 2012), https://hbr.org/2012/12/your-companys-history-as-a-leadership-tool.

2. Carol Dweck, "What Having a 'Growth Mindset' Actually Means," *Harvard Business Review* (January 13, 2016), https://hbr.org/2016/01/what-having-a-growth-mindset-actually-means.

3. Dweck, "What Having a 'Growth Mindset' Actually Means."

CHAPTER 30

1. Robert Kegan and Lisa Laskow Lahey, "Diagnosing Your Own Immunity to Change," excerpted from *Immunity to Change: How to Overcome It and Unlock Potential in Yourself and Your Organization* (Boston: Harvard Business Press, February 2015), https://mindsatwork.com/wp-content/uploads/2015/02/Chapter9.pdf.

2. Kegan and Lahey, "Diagnosing Your Own Immunity to Change."

CHAPTER 31

1. Described in their 2009 book, *Immunity to Change: How to Overcome It and Unlock the Potential in Yourself and Your Organization*, Robert Kegan and Lisa Laskow Lahey take a research-backed approach to explain how our mental patterns can cause us to make errors that block new information from coming in and prevent behavior changes. Changing mindsets may be the key to overcoming these mental barriers and embracing the changes we desire. MindTools offers steps and an interactive worksheet to overcome immunity to change (see https://www.mindtools.com/pages/article/immunity-to-change.htm).

PARTING WORDS

1. "Complacent," Dictionary.com, https://www.dictionary.com/browse/complacent.
2. "Toolbox Talk—Workplace Complacency," *Newfoundland & Labrador Construction Safety Association* (2018), http://www.nlcsa.com/downloads/Workplace%20Complacency%20TBT%20Final%202018.pdf.
3. Jill Lepore, "The Meaning of Life," *New Yorker*, May 14, 2007, https://www.newyorker.com/magazine/2007/05/21/the-meaning-of-life.
4. Lepore, "The Meaning of Life."
5. Brené Brown, *Rising Strong: The Reckoning. The Rumble. The Revolution* (New York: Random House, 2015).
6. Brown, *Rising Strong*, 18–19.
7. Fred Shapiro, "I Was Wrong about the Origin of the Serenity Prayer," HuffPost, May 15, 2014, https://www.huffpost.com/entry/serenity-prayer-origin_n_5331924.

Index

About the Authors

. . . .

An accomplished organizational leader in entrepreneurial arenas for the past 30 years, **Cleveland Justis** is a principal at Potrero Group, a management consulting organization with deep roots working in public-private partnerships, especially with state and national parks, land trusts, and social enterprises. Formerly, Cleveland was cofounder and director of the Institute at the Golden Gate and executive director of the Headlands Institute. He also led UC Davis's Institute for Innovation and Entrepreneurship. Cleveland has served in executive-level positions with the University of California, Golden Gate National Parks Conservancy, Headlands Institute of NatureBridge (formerly Yosemite National Institutes), and the National Outdoor Leadership School. Cleveland has held faculty positions at the UC Davis Graduate School of Management's MBA program, Georgetown University, and UC Berkeley's Haas Business School. He received his MBA in strategic management and finance at the UC Davis Graduate School of Management and earned his PhD in economic geography, entrepreneurship, and innovation at UC Davis. In his "downtime," Cleve is an active volunteer in the community. He served as a board member of the Marin Community Foundation, a large community foundation with over $2.3 billion in assets, and with Net Impact, an organization with a global network of over 15,000 leaders who are changing the world through business. Cleveland can be reached at cjustis@potrerogroup.com.

Daniel Student has been a cultural, environmental, and social sector leader for over 20 years and brings a unique cross-section of creative and business strategy to his work. He currently serves as a senior consultant for Potrero Group, working for amazing clients—including Outdoor Afro and Peninsula Open Space Trust—and, in perhaps his most proud example of not leading alone, providing program management for an inter-sector team for the development of California's "Pathways to 30x30" plan to conserve 30 percent of the state by 2030. He also regularly designs and leads workshops on teams, communication, culture, storytelling, leadership, and change management for conferences, organizations, and universities. His previous leadership positions included serving as producing artistic director for Plays & Players Theatre and administrative director for International Performing Arts for Youth. During that time of his life, he served as a theater director of over 30 plays, from which he draws facilitation and innovation skills to bring to his clients today and the storytelling chops to hopefully make this book a halfway decent read! You can learn more about Daniel and what he does at daniel-student.squarespace.com or just email him at dstudent@potrerogroup.com and say hi.

For more information and resources related to this book, please visit DontLeadAlone.com. To learn more about our consulting and executive search services, please visit potrerogroup.com.

Made in the USA
Coppell, TX
04 January 2024

27212991R00152